THE TAKEAWAY SECRET

How to Cook Your Favourite Fast Food at Home

D0988142

Also in Right Way

The Curry Secret
The New Curry Secret
An Indian Housewife's Recipe Book
Chinese Cookery Secrets
Thai Cookery Secrets

www.constablerobinson.com/rightway

THE TAKEAWAY SECRET

HOW TO COOK
YOUR FAVOURITE FAST FOOD
AT HOME

Kenny McGovern

RIGHT WAY

Constable & Robinson Ltd
3 The Lanchesters
162 Fulham Palace Road
London W6 9ER
www.constablerobinson.com

First published by Right Way, an imprint of Constable & Robinson, 2010

A copy of the British Library Cataloguing in Publication Data is available from
the British Library

ISBN: 978-0-7160-2235-0

Printed and bound in the EU
5 7 9 10 8 6

CONTENTS

INTRODUCTION

You are holding in your hands the result of years of trial and error, experimentation, and what can only be described as an almost unhealthy obsession with recreating takeaway and restaurant food. Over the years, hundreds of different recipes, ingredients and cooking methods have been tried and tested, the best of which are included in this book. Although I have always had a keen interest in cooking, I could never have known at the beginning of this process just how much of my life it would consume!

The book began life around eight years ago when I was 19 years old. Having worked as an IT assistant and office administrator for four years since leaving school at 16, I had found myself suffering panic attacks in the mornings on my way to work. This wasn't the first time I'd experienced such attacks, the first few had occurred in my school days when the walk to school often left me in a similar state of anxiety.

Having come to the conclusion that all was not as it should be, I arranged a doctor's appointment for later that week. As I arrived to attend my appointment, I wasn't entirely sure what I was doing at the doctor's surgery, or what I could tell the doctor about my situation. The only words that seemed to fit were 'something's just not right'. For many years, everyday social situations such as answering the telephone in front of work colleagues, attending meetings, or even travelling on public transport had left me in a state of high anxiety. On the outside, I appeared calm, confident even. On the inside, however, my heart would race and my mouth would become dry as I struggled with the most basic of situations.

I was diagnosed with Social Anxiety Disorder, an illness which puts people in a state of constant anxiety in social situations. While we all of course feel some nerves in certain social situations, such as giving a speech or trying to impress friends or work colleagues, in Social Anxiety sufferers these anxieties can appear to be switched on at all times, even when there is no reason or explanation for them. As the months passed, as is common with many Social Anxiety sufferers, I was diagnosed with secondary conditions of mild depression and agoraphobia as I struggled to make any progress in fighting the illness.

Having previously been an active person who had worked full time since leaving school, I found myself essentially housebound, reliant on family and friends to help me with everyday tasks such as grocery shopping. While this caused great difficulty in my life, and still does to this day, a somewhat flippant side effect of the situation also existed. Stuck at home, I quickly began to miss the simple luxuries of life which I'd previously been able to enjoy while at work or out socializing with friends. Simple pleasures like a fast-food cheeseburger, or a nice sandwich or baguette from the local bakery.

Before my illness prevented me from working, I had a particular lunchtime favourite: a simple sandwich topped with poppy seeds and filled with char grilled chicken pieces, lettuce, tomatoes and cucumbers; all fairly standard ingredients to prepare at home. One thing which was a little harder to recreate, however, was the honey and mustard mayonnaise dressing which covered the sandwich. It was this creamy sauce that made the sandwich so tasty, and so I grew ever frustrated at missing out on my lunchtime treat.

With a walk to the local bakery still proving extremely difficult, my attention turned to how to make this honey mustard mayonnaise dressing for myself. Not just something close, but something which exactly recreated the flavours and tastes I'd so enjoyed when eating the real thing. I began to look up recipes in books and online. Anyone I knew who had ever eaten from the bakery was quizzed intently on what they thought might be the ingredient providing that oh so special flavour. After some weeks, having been given advice from someone who had previously worked in the bakery in question, the secret recipe was obtained.

I knew the instant I tasted my latest sandwich attempt that I had indeed cracked it. The flavour was exactly as I remembered it, and so I was able to enjoy my favourite lunchtime sandwich once again. I was of course delighted and content with my success.

As the days and weeks passed, however, I found myself at a loss as to what to do next. So much of my time had been spent obsessing over the potential list of secret ingredients in my sandwich that I'd almost forgotten how to do anything but cook, or talk about cooking.

Before long, the excitement of finding out how to recreate similar dishes had taken hold. Mastering the flavours of one sandwich would not be enough, not with a whole world of fast-food and takeaway dishes out there just waiting to be made at home. And so the obsession began...

My thanks go to every takeaway chef or fast-food restaurant employee who's ever divulged their secrets to me (even those whose advice I'm still not sure wasn't designed to send me off track!). Thanks also to the many online friends who helpfully photographed their takeaway meals on my behalf and thought nothing of being asked to do so. I'll always appreciate how normal they made it feel to ask someone to photograph their takeaway dinner.

The highest praise of all has to be reserved for my girlfriend Rebecca, who along with my brother, sister and parents, has endured years of food related conversation. Their patience and encouragement were present in equal amounts throughout the writing of this book and my love and thanks will always be with them.

If you try the recipes included in this book, I hope you'll be glad to have done so.

1

THE TAKEAWAY SECRET

Takeaway and fast-food restaurants are an essential part of life, particularly in the modern world where time is ever more valuable. More and more of us are living such busy lives that it's very easy to find ourselves slipping into the 'takeaway routine'. Before we know it, that once-a-week treat can quickly become more frequent, ultimately proving to be very costly. What better compromise then than to create those same fantastic takeaway dishes at home, for a fraction of the cost.

After years of experimentation (and many, many conversations with takeaway chefs!), The Takeaway Secret can now be revealed. From classic American fast-food hamburgers to Indian curries and Chinese stir-fry, a huge selection of takeaway favourites can now be created with ease in any home kitchen. Like any good takeaway menu, I hope that there is something for everyone and a dish for all occasions.

Takeaway and fast-food items are cooked to order and so the majority of the recipes contained in this book are based around cooking one portion of each dish, except where circumstances make this impractical. The recipes are prepared and cooked with such ease, however, that scaling up to feed friends or family requires nothing more than cooking another portion to order, just as happens in your favourite fast-food restaurant.

In many cases, the cooking methods and ingredients used may differ slightly from those used by restaurant chefs. It's unlikely that home cooks will have access to such amazing cooking devices as tandoor ovens, kebab rotisseries, etc, and so an alternative cooking method must be found. Making the best of ingredients and equipment commonly available to the home cook, I hope that the recipes will provide quick, easy cooking and offer results which match or even improve on your takeaway favourites. The recipes in this book have been tested a variety of different ways, and the ingredients and cooking methods advised are those which have been found to provide the closest, most authentic takeaway experience.

All of the ingredients in this book are given in metric measurements with conversions listed where appropriate.

The recipes contained in the book will work equally well with slightly more or less of the main meat ingredient and so the cook should feel entirely comfortable using slightly smaller or larger chicken breast fillets, for example, should that be desired or should alternatives be unavailable. If you love your favourite takeaway curry but feel that the local restaurant could be a little more generous with the chunks of chicken, here's a chance to be extra generous to your guests by including a little more.

To take your homemade takeaway to another level, it's a good idea to purchase foil trays or plastic containers (you could, of course, use leftover containers from previous takeaway purchases!). As well as adding another level of authenticity to your meal, they also offer the added advantage of keeping your cooked food warm for a short while. This leaves ideal time to entertain your guests, or simply to put your feet up and relax after having prepared your food.

2

BURGERS

A well prepared hamburger with salad, sauces and fries is a complete meal in itself. Although all burgers share some similarities, there are a few subtle but important differences which should be observed when preparing a takeaway and fast-food style burger.

American fast-food burgers typically contain two unique ingredients which lend a special flavour to the prepared meal. Firstly, gherkins (or 'dill pickle'). When purchasing your jar of gherkins, ensure that dill is listed amongst the ingredients, as it's from this herb that the recognized American burger flavour will be obtained.

The second important ingredient in American fast-food burgers is yellow mustard. English and French mustards tend to have a far stronger flavour and will overpower the other flavours in your burger. Yellow mustard has a mellow, mild flavour, ideal to match with your burger. The best brand of American mustard to find is 'French's', not to be confused with French mustard!

Kebab shop style burgers are served with a much more tangible salad than their American fast-food cousin. Very finely sliced cabbage is added with the lettuce and a tangy topping based on spiced onions provides the sauce.

Although any good quality burger bun will suffice, the authentic takeaway experience can be more faithfully recreated by purchasing frozen sesame seed burger buns. These tend to be packaged in bags of 12 or 24 and can be purchased from any good frozen food supplier.

Tradition demands that French fries should be served with a classic American burger – preparing good French fries at home is a time-consuming task, and one which is rendered unnecessary by the high quality frozen products available nowadays from any good supermarket.

As indicated in the recipes, it is important to choose meat which has a relatively high fat content. The burgers are cooked without any added fat, and some of the fat contained within the meat will be lost during the cooking process. Starting with a lean meat will result in dry, tough burgers, while using meat with a higher fat content will ensure the cooked burgers remain moist and juicy.

HAMBURGER

(AMERICAN FAST-FOOD STYLE)

Serves 1

Roughly 56 g/2 oz beef mince (minimum 20% fat)
1 burger bun
Pinch of salt and pinch of black pepper
½ tablespoon tomato ketchup (recommended brand: Heinz)
1 teaspoon yellow mustard (recommended brand: French's)
1 teaspoon finely chopped onion
2 thin slices of gherkin
1 processed cheese slice (optional)

Roll the beef mince into a ball. Using a sheet of greaseproof paper, flatten the mince into a thin, circular patty, slightly bigger than the size of your burger bun. Cover and place in the coldest part of the fridge for 1–2 hours.

Heat a dry, flat frying pan to a medium heat. Toast the burger buns face down in the pan for around 30 seconds or until golden. Set aside.

Place the burger patty onto the hot, dry pan and cook for 60–90 seconds. Apply very gentle pressure with a spatula to ensure even browning.

Flip the burger. Add a pinch of salt and black pepper and cook for a further 60 seconds, or until cooked through and juices run clear.

Place five dots of ketchup on the inside of the top bun, like the '5' on a dice. Add five smaller drops of yellow mustard between the ketchup. Add a pinch of finely chopped onion and the two gherkin slices. Add the cheese slice if desired.

Place the burger patty onto the dressed burger bun. Add the bottom bun. Wrap the burger in foil or baking paper and place in the oven at the lowest available setting for 3–4 minutes to combine flavours and heat through. Serve with French fries.

QUARTER POUNDER BURGER

(AMERICAN FAST-FOOD STYLE)

Serves 1

Roughly 113 g/4 oz beef mince (minimum 20% fat)
1 large burger bun
Pinch of salt and pinch of black pepper
1 tablespoon tomato ketchup (recommended brand: Heinz)
2 teaspoons yellow mustard (recommended brand: French's)
1 tablespoon finely chopped onion
4 thin slices of gherkin
1 processed cheese slice (optional)

Roll the beef mince into a ball. Using a sheet of greaseproof paper, flatten the mince into a thin, circular patty, slightly bigger than the size of your burger bun. Cover and place in the coldest part of the fridge for 1–2 hours.

Heat a dry, flat frying pan to a medium-high heat. Toast the burger buns face down in the pan for around 30 seconds or until golden. Set aside. Place the burger patty onto the hot, dry pan and cook for 2–3 minutes. Apply very gentle pressure with a spatula to ensure even browning.

Flip the burger. Add a pinch of salt and black pepper and cook for a further 2 minutes, or until cooked through and juices run clear.

Place five large dots of ketchup on the inside of the top bun, like the '5' on a dice. Add five smaller drops of yellow mustard between the ketchup. Add a large pinch of finely chopped onion and the four gherkin slices. Add the cheese slice if desired.

Place the burger patty onto the dressed burger bun. Add the bottom bun. Wrap the burger in foil or baking paper and place in the oven at the lowest available setting for 3–4 minutes to combine flavours and heat through. Serve with French fries.

QUARTER POUNDER BURGER

(Kebab Shop Style)

Serves 1

Roughly 113 g/4 oz beef mince (minimum 20% fat)
1 large burger bun
Pinch of salt
Pinch of black pepper
¼ small onion, diced
2 tablespoons tomato ketchup
½ teaspoon mint sauce
1 small handful of shredded lettuce
1 small handful of shredded white cabbage
1 tomato slice
1 processed cheese slice (optional)

Roll the beef mince into a ball. Using a sheet of greaseproof paper, flatten the mince into a thin, circular patty, slightly bigger than the size of your burger bun. Cover and place in the coldest part of the fridge for 1–2 hours.

Heat a griddle pan to a medium-high heat. Toast the burger buns face down in the pan for around 30 seconds or until golden. Set aside. Place the burger patty onto the hot, dry griddle pan and cook for 2–3 minutes. Apply very gentle pressure with a spatula to ensure even browning.

Flip the burger. Add a pinch of salt and black pepper and cook for a further 2 minutes, or until cooked through and juices run clear.

Combine the onion with the tomato ketchup and mint sauce. Dress the top bun with a tablespoon of the mixture. Add a handful of shredded lettuce, cabbage and tomato slice. On the bottom bun, add the processed cheese slice if desired.

Place the cooked burger patty onto the top burger bun. Add the bottom bun. Wrap the burger loosely in foil or baking paper and place in the oven at the lowest available setting for 3–4 minutes to combine flavours and heat through. Serve with French fries.

LAMB BURGER

(KEBAB SHOP STYLE)

Serves 1

Roughly 113 g/4 oz lamb mince (minimum 20% fat)
¼ small onion, finely chopped
¼ teaspoon cumin powder
Small handful of fresh coriander leaves, finely chopped
Pinch of salt
Pinch of black pepper
1 large burger bun
1 tablespoon tzatziki or raita to serve

In a large bowl, combine the lamb mince, chopped onion, cumin powder, fresh coriander, salt and pepper. Mix thoroughly until all of the ingredients are distributed evenly throughout the meat.

Roll the lamb mixture into a ball. Using a sheet of greaseproof paper, flatten the mixture into a thin, circular patty, slightly bigger than the size of your burger bun. Cover and place in the coldest part of the fridge for 1–2 hours.

Heat a griddle pan to a medium-high heat. Toast the burger buns face down in the pan for around 30 seconds or until golden. Set aside. Place the lamb burger patty onto the hot, dry griddle pan and cook for 2–3 minutes. Apply very gentle pressure with a spatula to ensure even browning.

Flip the burger and cook for a further 2 minutes, or until cooked through and juices run clear.

Place the cooked burger patty onto the top burger bun. Garnish with 1 tablespoon of tzatziki or raita. Add the bottom bun, flip and serve with Pitta Salad (page 123) and French fries.

MEGA BURGER

(AMERICAN FAST-FOOD STYLE)

Serves 1

This classic burger has an added bread layer in the middle and two burger patties, served with the famous Special Burger Sauce.

Roughly 113 g/4 oz beef mince (minimum 20% fat)
1 burger bun and 1 bottom half burger bun
Pinch of salt
Pinch of black pepper
2 tablespoons Special Burger Sauce
2 teaspoons finely chopped onion
1 small handful of shredded iceberg lettuce
4 thin slices of gherkin
1 processed cheese slice

Roll the beef mince into two balls. Using a sheet of greaseproof paper, flatten the mince into two thin, circular patties, slightly bigger than the size of your burger bun. Cover and place in the coldest part of the fridge for 1–2 hours.

Heat a dry, flat frying pan to a medium–high heat. Toast the burger buns face down in the pan for around 30 seconds or until golden. Set aside. Place the burger patties onto the hot, dry pan and cook for 2 minutes. Apply very gentle pressure with a spatula to ensure even browning.

Flip the burgers. Add a pinch of salt and black pepper and cook for a further 2 minutes, or until cooked through and juices run clear. If necessary, cook the burgers one at a time and keep warm in the oven at the lowest available setting until required.

Dress the bottom and middle layer buns with a tablespoon of Special Burger Sauce. Add a teaspoon of finely chopped onion and a handful of shredded iceberg lettuce. On the middle bun, place two gherkin slices. On the bottom bun, add the processed cheese slice.

Place the burger patties onto the dressed buns. Carefully lift the middle layer and place it on top of the bottom layer. Add the top burger bun. Wrap the burger loosely in foil or baking paper and place in the oven at the lowest available setting for 3–4 minutes to combine flavours and heat through. Serve with French fries.

SPECIAL BURGER SAUCE

(AMERICAN FAST-FOOD STYLE)

Makes enough sauce for 3 Mega Burgers

This world-famous burger sauce is an essential mega burger ingredient, but also works well with hot dogs or as a sandwich dressing.

4 tablespoons mayonnaise (recommended brand: Hellman's)
2 teaspoons yellow mustard (recommended brand: French's)
2 teaspoons tomato ketchup (recommended brand: Heinz)
1 tablespoon finely chopped gherkin

In a small bowl, combine the mayonnaise, yellow mustard and ketchup. Add the chopped gherkin and mix well. Refrigerate for at least 1 hour before use.

PHILLY CHEESE STEAK

(AMERICAN FAST-FOOD STYLE)

Serves 1

The key to this sandwich is to ensure the steak is sliced as thinly as possible, enabling extremely quick cooking and juicy, tender steak pieces for your finished sandwich. American customers often include 'cheeze whiz', a processed cheese product. Provolone or even Mozzarella will also work well in this sandwich. The debate over which type of cheese should be used is fierce, so feel free to use whichever is your favourite. Optional additions to this sandwich include green peppers, mushrooms, chilli sauce, pizza sauce or mayonnaise.

Roughly 113 g/4 oz sirloin beef steak
2 tablespoons vegetable oil
1 onion, thinly sliced
Pinch of salt and pepper
1 sub roll, hot dog roll or French baguette
1 processed cheese slice

Slice the sirloin steak as thinly as possible into thin strips. Place in a bowl with 1 tablespoon of the vegetable oil.

Heat a dry, flat frying pan to a medium heat. Place the remaining tablespoon of vegetable oil in the pan. Add the sliced onion to the pan and cook for 8–10 minutes or until the onion begins to darken and become crisp.

Increase the heat to high and add the steak. Season with a little salt and pepper, then stir-fry for 2–3 minutes or until the steak is just cooked through.

Slice open the roll and fill with the cooked onion and steak. Cut the processed cheese slice into strips and add to the roll. Place in a warm oven for 3–4 minutes to allow the cheese to melt. Serve with ketchup or yellow mustard if desired.

CHICKEN FILLET BURGER

(AMERICAN FAST-FOOD STYLE)

Serves 1

1 tablespoon vegetable oil
100 ml/3½ fl oz water
3 tablespoons tomato ketchup (recommended brand: Heinz)
½ teaspoon dried Italian herbs
¼ teaspoon paprika
Pinch of onion powder
Pinch of salt
Pinch of black pepper
¼ teaspoon liquid smoke (optional but recommended)
1 small skinless, boneless chicken breast fillet (around
   85 g/3 oz weight)
1 burger bun
1 tablespoon mayonnaise (recommended brand: Hellman's)
1 handful of shredded lettuce
2 large tomato slices

In a bowl or food-safe bag, combine the vegetable oil, water, tomato ketchup, Italian herbs, paprika, onion powder, salt, black pepper and liquid smoke.

Using a meat mallet, pound the chicken breast fillet until thin. Use scissors to shape the chicken piece to your burger bun. Add to the bowl or food bag and marinade for at least 4 hours, or overnight if possible.

Heat a griddle pan on a medium–high heat. Toast the buns face down on the griddle pan for around 30 seconds or until golden. Remove and set aside.

Place the chicken onto the hot griddle pan. Cook for 3–4 minutes. Turn the chicken and continue to cook for another 3–4 minutes or until the chicken is cooked through.

Dress the top burger bun with mayonnaise, shredded lettuce and tomato slices. Place the cooked chicken piece on top and serve with French fries.

CHICKEN SANDWICH BURGER

(AMERICAN FAST-FOOD STYLE)

Serves 1

120 g/4 oz plain flour
1 teaspoon onion powder
½ teaspoon garlic powder
1 teaspoon salt and ½ teaspoon black pepper
1 egg
120 ml/4 fl oz milk
1 small skinless, boneless chicken breast fillet (around
    85 g/3 oz weight)
1 burger bun
Oil for deep frying
Pinch of onion powder
1 tablespoon mayonnaise
Handful of shredded lettuce

In a bowl, combine the plain flour, onion powder, garlic powder, salt and black pepper. In a separate bowl, combine the egg and milk.

Trim any excess fat from the chicken breast fillet. Using a meat mallet, pound the chicken breast fillet until thin. Use scissors to shape the chicken piece to fit the burger bun. Keeping one hand dry, dip the chicken piece first into the seasoned flour, then into the egg and milk mixture, and finally into the seasoned flour once again. Leave to rest for a few minutes and repeat the process again.

Heat a dry, flat frying pan to a medium heat. Toast the buns face down in the pan for around 30 seconds or until golden. Set aside.

Deep fry the chicken burger in hot oil on a medium heat for around 5–6 minutes or until golden brown and cooked through. Remove the chicken from the pan and drain off any excess oil.

Mix the pinch of onion powder through the tablespoon of mayonnaise. Dress the top burger bun with the mayonnaise mixture and top with shredded lettuce. Place the cooked chicken piece on top. Add the bottom bun and serve with French fries.

FISH FILLET BURGER

(American Fast-Food Style)

Serves 1

Hoki was the traditional choice of fish fillet for sandwiches for many years in American restaurants, but recently Alaskan pollock has become more widely used. Any firm white fish will provide good results.

3–4 tablespoons plain flour
¼ teaspoon salt
¼ teaspoon black pepper
1 egg
6 tablespoons milk
2 slices of white bread, crusts removed
1 small white fish fillet
2–3 tablespoons oil
1 burger bun
1 tablespoon tartar sauce
½ processed cheese slice

In a bowl, combine the plain flour, salt and black pepper. Mix well. In a separate bowl, combine the egg and milk. Whisk thoroughly. Add the bread slices to a blender. Blitz well. Pour the breadcrumbs into a bowl and set aside. Trim the fish fillet to fit the burger bun.

Keeping one hand dry, dip the fish fillet first into the seasoned flour, then into the egg and milk mixture, and finally into the breadcrumbs. Set the breaded fish aside in the fridge for 1 hour. This will help the breadcrumb coating to stick to the fish.

Heat a dry, flat frying pan to a medium heat. Toast the buns face down in the pan for around 30 seconds or until golden. Set aside.

Fry the breaded fish fillet in a few tablespoons of oil on a medium heat for around 5–6 minutes or until golden and cooked through. Turn the fish once during cooking.

Dress the top burger bun with the tartar sauce. Add the cooked fish and place the cheese slice on top. Add the bottom bun. Serve with French fries.

3

KEBABS

Kebabs of one kind or another are eaten all around the world. The word 'kebab' is Turkish in origin and it's often suggested that this style of food was invented by medieval fighters who used their swords as skewers, holding pieces of meat over an open flame. In truth, kebabs reflect cooking in its simplest terms. Even as modern technology introduces various new kitchen tools and gadgets, the simplicity and depth of flavour offered when cooking marinated meats over an open flame cannot be beaten. In any country, good weather offers the chance to eat outdoors and kebabs are the number one barbecue choice.

For most home cooks, the chance to cook outdoors over an open flame comes around all too infrequently. For that reason, alternative cooking methods must be found which best recreate the same flavours and aromas associated with good kebabs. The cooking methods used in this chapter will offer excellent results; however do experiment with your barbecue or charcoal grill should the weather be kind enough to allow it.

The classic 'Lamb Doner' kebab is perhaps the most commonly eaten fast-food kebab in the western world. It has gained a somewhat unfortunate reputation over time, with many critics pointing to high levels of salt and fat within poor quality takeaway offerings. Although not without some truth, these stories do not do justice to the high quality kebabs which are available from some of the country's most talented takeaway restaurant chefs. In many parts of the world, good kebabs are eaten not only as a late night snack, but also as a healthy, nutritious lunch or dinner. Using fresh meat and spices, marinated over time to intensify the flavours, the chef creates a meal which is both healthy and delicious. By creating your own kebabs in the same way with the recipes contained in this chapter, you'll be sure of capturing that authentic kebab flavour in the healthiest way possible.

The recipes included here should of course be served with a selection of flatbreads, salads and sauces. Traditionally, kebabs are served with pitta bread. In recent times, an alternative choice known as a 'King Kebab' has been added to many takeaway menus. This dish resembles a traditional kebab in almost every way; however, it is often slightly larger in size and is accompanied by nan bread as opposed to pitta.

LAMB DONER KEBAB

(KEBAB SHOP STYLE)

Serves 3–4

Traditionally the lamb doner kebab is cooked on a standing rotisserie and thinly sliced to order. The thin slices are perfect because the meat is generously seasoned. This home version is roasted in the oven and uses a classic doner spice mix to capture that authentic takeaway flavour.

1 teaspoon plain flour
1 teaspoon dried oregano
½ teaspoon dried Italian herbs
½ teaspoon garlic powder
½ teaspoon onion powder
¼ teaspoon cayenne pepper
1 teaspoon salt
½ teaspoon black pepper
500 g/1.1 lb lamb mince

Preheat the oven to 180°C/350°F/Gas Mark 4.

In a large bowl, combine the plain flour, dried oregano, dried Italian herbs, garlic powder, onion powder, cayenne pepper, salt and black pepper.

Add the lamb mince and mix thoroughly for 2–3 minutes. Take out all of your aggression on the kebab mixture, punching and kneading until no air pockets remain and the kebab meat is extremely smooth.

Shape the seasoned mince into a loaf and place on a baking tray.

Bake in the middle shelf of the oven for 1 hour 20 minutes, turning the loaf half way through the cooking time to ensure even browning.

Once cooked, remove from the oven and cover with foil. Allow to rest for 10 minutes.

Slice the doner kebab as thinly as possible and serve with Pitta Salad (page 123) and kebab sauces.

LAMB SHISH KEBAB

(KEBAB SHOP STYLE)

Serves 1–2

50 ml/2 fl oz olive oil
1 tablespoon Worcester sauce
2 tablespoons lemon juice
¼ onion
2 cloves of garlic
1 teaspoon cumin powder
½ teaspoon smoked paprika
1 teaspoon dried oregano
½ teaspoon dried rosemary
¼ teaspoon black pepper
250 g/½ lb boneless lamb leg steak

In a blender, combine the olive oil, Worcester sauce, lemon juice, onion, garlic, cumin powder, smoked paprika, dried oregano, dried rosemary and black pepper.

Trim any excess fat from the lamb leg steak and cut into several medium-large pieces. In a bowl or food-safe bag, add the lamb and blended ingredients. Mix well and marinade for at least 4 hours, or overnight if possible.

Preheat the oven to 200°C/400°F/Gas Mark 6.

Arrange the lamb pieces on a wire rack over a roasting tray and bake on the highest oven shelf for 10 minutes.

Turn the lamb pieces and bake for a further 6 minutes.

Turn the lamb pieces once more and bake for a further 3–4 minutes or until just beginning to char.

Remove the lamb and set aside on a plate or serving dish to rest for 2–3 minutes. Serve with Pitta Salad (page 123) and kebab sauces.

LAMB KOFTA KEBAB

(Kebab Shop Style)

Serves 3–4

500 g/1.1 lb lamb mince
1 medium onion, grated or very finely chopped
1 clove of garlic, finely chopped
2 finger chilli peppers, very finely chopped (see page 39)
¼ teaspoon allspice
½ teaspoon sweet paprika
½ teaspoon cumin powder
½ teaspoon salt
¼ teaspoon black pepper
1 egg

In a bowl, combine the lamb mince, onion, garlic, chilli peppers, allspice, sweet paprika, cumin powder, salt and black pepper.

Crack the egg into the bowl and mix well. As with the doner kebab, punch the kebab mixture well and mix thoroughly for 2–3 minutes or until extremely smooth.

Divide the kofta mixture into 10–12 pieces. Using wet hands shape each piece into sausage shapes. Press down gently in the middle of each kofta.

Heat a little oil in a griddle or frying pan over a medium-high heat. When the pan is hot, add the kofta pieces and cook for around 8–10 minutes or until cooked through and golden. Turn the koftas occasionally during cooking.

Serve with Pitta Salad (page 123) and kebab sauces.

SEEKH KEBAB

(Kebab Shop Style)

Serves 1–2

½ small onion
½ green finger chilli pepper (see page 39)
1 teaspoon garlic and ginger paste
½ teaspoon cumin powder
½ teaspoon coriander powder
½ teaspoon paprika
Pinch of cayenne pepper
¼ teaspoon salt
1 small handful of fresh coriander
1 small handful of fresh mint
250 g/½ lb beef mince

In a blender or pestle and mortar, combine the onion, chilli pepper, garlic and ginger paste, cumin powder, coriander powder, paprika, cayenne pepper, salt, fresh coriander and fresh mint. Blend well for 1–2 minutes, scraping the side of the blender occasionally until the ingredients are fully combined.

Pour the blended mixture into a large bowl. Add the beef mince and mix thoroughly until fully combined.

Using wet hands, divide the mixture into 3–4 sausage shapes. The kebabs can be shaped around skewers if desired.

Preheat the oven to 200°C/400°F/Gas Mark 6. Arrange the kebabs on a wire rack over a roasting tray and bake for around 6 minutes.

Turn the kebabs to ensure even browning. Bake for a further 6 minutes.

Finish the kebabs under a hot grill or on a griddle pan, cooking for a further 3–4 minutes or until just charred on each side.

Serve with Pitta Salad (page 123) and kebab sauces.

CHICKEN DONER KEBAB

(KEBAB SHOP STYLE)

Serves 1

2 tablespoons olive oil
1 tablespoon tomato purée
4 tablespoons lemon juice
¼ teaspoon garlic powder
¼ teaspoon onion powder
¼ teaspoon cumin powder
¼ teaspoon salt
¼ teaspoon black pepper
2 medium skinless, boneless chicken thighs (around
  113 g/4 oz total weight)
2 lemon slices

In a large bowl or food-safe bag, add the olive oil, tomato purée, lemon juice, garlic powder, onion powder, cumin powder, salt and black pepper.

Trim any excess fat from the chicken thighs and cut into small, thin pieces. Add the chicken pieces to the marinade and mix well. Marinade for at least 4 hours, or overnight if possible.

Heat a dry, flat frying pan to a high heat. Drop the chicken pieces into the pan and leave untouched for 1 minute.

Turn the chicken pieces and continue to fry for a further 4–5 minutes, stirring occasionally. Fry the chicken in batches if necessary, leaving enough room in the pan for the chicken pieces to fry at a high heat. When each batch is cooked, set aside in the oven at the lowest available setting to keep warm until all of the chicken is ready.

When all of the chicken pieces are cooked, arrange on a plate and garnish with lemon slices. Serve with Pitta Salad (page 123) and kebab sauces.

CHICKEN BARBECUE KEBAB

(KEBAB SHOP STYLE)

Serves 1

If fresh lemon juice is used in this recipe, thin slices of lemon can be placed on top of the chicken pieces during cooking to add moisture.

2 tablespoons olive oil
2 tablespoons lemon juice
1 tablespoon Worcester sauce
½ teaspoon garlic powder
½ teaspoon onion powder
¼ teaspoon paprika
¼ teaspoon salt
¼ teaspoon black pepper
1 large skinless, boneless chicken breast fillet (around
    113 g/4 oz weight)

In a large bowl or food-safe bag, add the olive oil, lemon juice, Worcester sauce, garlic powder, onion powder, paprika, salt and black pepper.

Trim any excess fat from the chicken breast and cut into 5–6 pieces. Add the chicken pieces to the marinade and mix well. Marinade for at least 4 hours, or overnight if possible.

Heat a dry griddle pan to a medium–high heat. Place the chicken pieces onto the griddle and leave for 2 minutes.

Continue cooking the chicken for a further 4–5 minutes, turning occasionally until golden on all sides and cooked through.

Serve with Pitta Salad (page 123) and kebab sauces.

CHICKEN SHASHLIK KEBAB

(KEBAB SHOP STYLE)

Serves 1–2

2 tablespoons vegetable oil
2 tablespoons lemon juice
¼ teaspoon paprika
¼ teaspoon ginger powder
¼ teaspoon garlic powder
½ teaspoon cumin powder
¼ teaspoon garam masala
¼ teaspoon sugar
Small handful of fresh coriander, finely chopped
Pinch of salt and pinch of black pepper
1 large skinless, boneless chicken breast fillet (around
    113 g/4 oz weight)
1 onion, chopped into large pieces
1 green pepper, chopped into large pieces

In a large bowl or food-safe bag, add the vegetable oil, lemon juice, paprika, ginger powder, garlic powder, cumin powder, garam masala, sugar, fresh coriander, salt and pepper.

Trim any excess fat from the chicken breast and cut into small, thin pieces. Add the chicken pieces to the marinade and mix well. Marinade for at least 4 hours, or overnight if possible.

Preheat the oven to 200°C/400°F/Gas Mark 6.

Arrange the chicken pieces on a wire rack over a roasting tray and bake for 8 minutes. Turn the chicken pieces and return to the oven for a further 8 minutes. Turn the chicken pieces once more and bake for a further 2–3 minutes or until just beginning to char.

When the chicken pieces are almost cooked, heat a little vegetable oil in a frying pan over a medium heat. Add the chopped onion and green pepper and stir-fry for 5–6 minutes.

Arrange the chicken on a plate or serving tray and add the cooked onion and green pepper. Serve with Pitta Salad (page 123) and kebab sauces.

4

THE CHIP SHOP

For many years chip shops dominated the takeaway market in the UK and they are still extremely popular today. A properly prepared fish supper is healthier than you might imagine too. By frying the fish at a high heat, the batter is trapped around the fish, allowing the fillet to steam inside until just cooked through. Good chip shop food shouldn't taste too greasy; if it does the chances are that the oil has not been hot enough during cooking.

Although haddock and cod are the traditional chip shop choice, any white fish can be used so do experiment. With your fish batter prepared, any number of food items may be battered and deep-fried for an occasional unhealthy treat, including Mars bars if desired!

For an even more authentic takeaway experience, serve your fish and chips with a portion of mushy peas and plenty of salt and vinegar. Many people find that supermarket brand vinegars taste different from that found in chip shops; when shopping for vinegar to go with your chips, look for a product called 'Non Brewed Condiment'. Many chip shops use this vinegar substitute, made from water, acetic acid and caramel colour.

FISH IN BATTER
(Chip Shop Style)

Serves 1

Sparkling water or any good beer will also work well instead of water in the batter mixture. The key to good battered fish is to ensure the oil is sufficiently hot before frying. If the oil is not hot enough, the batter will become greasy.

120 g/4 oz plain flour
1 teaspoon baking powder
½ teaspoon salt
60 ml/2 fl oz water
1 tablespoon white vinegar
1 egg
1 large haddock or cod fillet
Pinch of salt
Pinch of pepper
2 tablespoons plain flour

In a large bowl, combine the plain flour, baking powder and salt.

Slowly add the water until a thick batter begins to form. Add the white vinegar and egg and mix thoroughly.

Add more water until the batter becomes smooth with the consistency of single cream.

Season the fish fillet with a little salt and pepper. Coat in the plain flour and dip into the batter mixture. Drain off any excess batter and place carefully into the hot oil.

Deep fry on a medium–high heat for 5–6 minutes or until the fish is cooked through and the batter is golden and crispy.

Remove the fish from the pan and drain off any excess oil. Season with salt and vinegar and serve with chips and mushy peas.

CHIP SHOP CHIPS
(Chip Shop Style)

Serves 1

Maris Piper or King Edward potatoes will produce by far the best results when making chips. This method takes a little time but delivers good results and allows the home cook to prepare chips in advance and finish them off in batches when hungry guests are ready to eat.

200–250 g/8 oz potatoes per person
Vegetable oil for deep frying

Peel the potatoes and slice into 1cm/½ inch thick chips. Wash the chips thoroughly in cold water for 1–2 minutes.

Fill a large pan with water and bring to the boil. Add the chips and simmer for 3–4 minutes. Remove the chips from the water and drain thoroughly. Set aside to cool.

Heat the vegetable oil over a medium heat. Add the chips in small batches and fry for a few minutes until the chips just begin to soften. Remove the chips from the pan before they begin to take on any colour.

Drain excess oil from the chips. Set aside in the refrigerator until cold or until ready for use.

Heat the vegetable oil over a medium-high heat. Add the chips in batches once again and fry for 5–6 minutes more, or until the chips have turned golden and crisp.

Remove from the pan, drain off any excess oil and serve with salt and vinegar.

POTATO FRITTERS

(CHIP SHOP STYLE)

Serves 2–3

120 g/4 oz plain flour
1 teaspoon baking powder
½ teaspoon salt
60 ml/2 fl oz water
1 tablespoon white vinegar
1 egg
2 large potatoes, peeled and thickly sliced
2 tablespoons plain flour

In a large bowl, combine the plain flour, baking powder and salt.

Slowly add the water until a thick batter begins to form. Add the white vinegar and egg and mix thoroughly.

Add more water until the batter becomes smooth with the consistency of single cream.

Preheat the oven to 180°C/350°F/Gas Mark 4.

Coat the potato slices in the flour and dip into the batter mixture. Deep fry the fritters on a medium-high heat for 3–4 minutes or until the batter is sealed and the fritters are just beginning to change colour.

Remove the fritters from the pan and drain off any excess oil. Arrange the potato fritters on a wire rack over a roasting tray and place into the oven for 10–12 minutes or until the potato is soft and cooked through and the batter is golden.

Season with salt and vinegar and serve with a crispy roll.

5

INDIAN MAIN MEALS

Indian takeaway food continues to grow in popularity thanks to the sheer variety of dishes on the menu. From mild, creamy Korma to hotter dishes such as South Indian Garlic Chilli Chicken, there is a curry to suit all tastes. The wide range of Indian starters and side dishes is also extremely popular, with many of these items now appearing on kebab shop menus around the country.

Don't be put off by the number of spices and ingredients required in Indian cooking. With a little experience, use of spices becomes as easy as knowing how much salt and pepper to add to your dish. Filling a kitchen store cupboard with spices will prove to be a very worthwhile investment, adding a delicious Indian twist to any meal.

In order to best replicate the flavours found in takeaway restaurant curries, it's a good idea to purchase branded spices where possible. The spices most frequently used in restaurants are: TRS; East End; Rajah.

While other brands of spices can be used, and will produce excellent results, a more authentic flavour can be obtained by sourcing spices from these companies. If possible, try to stick to one brand; so for example if you use TRS chilli powder, try to ensure all other spices used in your curry are TRS spices. This is important, but certainly not essential so please don't let it put you off trying the recipes included in this chapter.

Although the initial preparation in creating your own Indian curry can seem a little time-consuming, the rewards make the process very worthwhile. Within a couple of hours, you can stock a freezer full of ingredients ready for use in the months ahead. With these items prepared, you can cook your favourite curry in around 10 minutes. The nan bread and chapatti recipes included in this book also freeze very well, leaving you with little to do in order to create a full Indian feast.

Indian restaurant cooking is perhaps closer to Chinese stir-frying than the traditional curry. As opposed to stewing curry dishes over a long period of time, the restaurant uses a single curry stock or gravy for each dish, adding specific individual flavours during the last minutes of the dish's preparation. Using this method, any curry on the menu can be created in around ten minutes.

When cooking your curry, it is crucial that the spices cook, but do not burn. Getting this right can take a little practice. One common mistake is to cook the spices on too high a heat. While restaurant chefs do often use very high temperatures, it's all too easy for the home cook to overdo things at the spices stage. Scraping the pan is one good way to ensure your spices cook without burning. When the spices are cooked correctly, they will begin to foam in the pan. If you're worried about burning your spices, add a touch of water to the pan whenever a recipe calls for spices to be added. With time, you'll become used to the heat your stovetop offers and be able to increase the heat as desired. Another handy tip is to measure out the required spices for each curry ahead of time. This enables you to add the spices quickly and continue cooking without interruption. As with any meal, advance preparation will make the final cooking process easy.

Chicken or Lamb Tikka are perfect to cook ahead and use in finished curries and offer the easiest and quickest cooking method. Many restaurants or takeaways will use less expensive cuts of beef or lamb which require longer cooking before use in the finished curry. This can be done at home using the recipe included in this chapter. Cooked meat will freeze well for up to three months.

Be careful when preparing fresh chillies as the irritant in them causes a burning sensation when in contact with the skin. So wash your hands thoroughly after touching them.

BASIC CURRY SAUCE

(INDIAN RESTAURANT STYLE)

Makes enough Basic Curry Sauce for 7–8 Curries

This curry sauce can be frozen in batches and used in a diverse range of finished curry dishes. With the basic curry sauce prepared and ready for use, any of the curry dishes in this chapter can be created in around 10 minutes.

75 ml/2½ fl oz vegetable oil
2 carrots, chopped
1½ large Spanish onions (around 700 g/1½ lb peeled weight), chopped
½ green pepper, chopped
2½ litres/4½ pints water
2 tablespoons tomato purée
1 tablespoon garlic and ginger paste
1 teaspoon coriander powder
1 teaspoon cumin powder
1 teaspoon turmeric powder
½ tablespoon garam masala
1 large handful of chopped fresh coriander leaves and stalks
200 g tinned chopped tomatoes
25 g/1 oz creamed coconut block
¼ teaspoon salt

Heat the oil in a large stock pot and add the vegetables. Stir-fry over a medium heat for 5–6 minutes.

Add the water, tomato purée, garlic and ginger paste, coriander powder, cumin powder, turmeric, garam masala, fresh coriander, tinned tomatoes, creamed coconut block and salt.

Bring the pan back to the boil on a high heat. Once boiling, reduce the heat to medium-low. Simmer for 1 hour.

Using a hand blender, blitz the sauce. Continue blending for 2–3 minutes until no vegetable pieces remain and the sauce is completely smooth.

Return the pan to the heat and simmer for a further 15 minutes. Add a little more water if necessary. The finished sauce should have the consistency of a thin soup.

Allow the sauce to cool and pour into freezer safe storage tubs. Freeze in 200–300ml/7–10 fl oz batches for up to 3 months. Each batch will provide enough basic curry sauce for 1 portion of curry.

CURRY STOCK LAMB

(INDIAN RESTAURANT STYLE)

This stock will result in tender chunks of meat with a mild flavour which can be stored and used with any of the curry recipes in this chapter. The advantage this offers is that less expensive, stewing cuts of meat may be used in curry dishes if desired. The recipe may be doubled or even tripled if a large amount of meat is to be precooked.

3 tablespoons vegetable oil
1 teaspoon garlic and ginger paste
300 ml/10½ fl oz Basic Curry Sauce (page 40)
300 ml/10½ fl oz water
¼ teaspoon coriander powder
¼ teaspoon cumin powder
¼ teaspoon turmeric
¼ teaspoon salt
2 x 400 g/14 oz packs lamb leg steaks (4–6 steaks,
    800 g/2 lb in total), prepared as below

In a large pan, heat the vegetable oil over a medium heat. Add the garlic and ginger paste. Stir-fry for 1 minute.

Add the basic curry sauce and water. Mix well.

Add the coriander powder, cumin powder, turmeric and salt. Mix well and bring the pan to boiling point.

Trim any excess fat from the lamb and cut into large pieces. Add to the pan, reduce the heat to a simmer and cook for around 1 hour, or until the meat is tender. Add a little more water if required during cooking to ensure the meat remains covered.

Drain the stock and reserve the cooked meat. Use immediately or allow to cool and freeze in batches of 7–8 pieces for use in any curry dish.

TANDOORI CHICKEN

(INDIAN RESTAURANT STYLE)

Serves 2

5–6 chicken pieces (thighs and drumsticks), skin removed
1 tablespoon vegetable oil
2 tablespoons lemon juice
1 teaspoon chilli pepper
1 teaspoon salt
250 ml/9 fl oz natural yogurt
1 teaspoon garlic and ginger paste
1 teaspoon garam masala
¼ teaspoon paprika
¼ teaspoon coriander powder
¼ teaspoon cumin powder
1–2 drops of natural red food colour (optional)

Pierce the chicken thighs and drumsticks in several places with a fork. Add the vegetable oil, lemon juice, chilli pepper and salt. Rub the mixture into the chicken thoroughly and set aside in the fridge for 1 hour.

Add the natural yogurt, garlic and ginger paste, garam masala, paprika, coriander powder, cumin powder and natural red food colour to the chicken pieces. Mix well once again and set aside in the fridge for 3–4 hours or overnight if possible.

Preheat the oven to 220°C/425°F/Gas Mark 7.

Arrange the tandoori chicken pieces on a wire rack over a roasting tray and bake on the middle shelf for 9 minutes.

Turn the tandoori pieces and bake for a further 9 minutes. Turn the tandoori pieces once more and bake for a further 9 minutes or until the chicken is cooked through, the juices run clear and the thighs and drumsticks are just beginning to char.

Serve the tandoori chicken pieces as a kebab with Pitta Salad (page 123) or nan bread.

TRADITIONAL CHICKEN CURRY

(INDIAN RESTAURANT STYLE)

Serves 1–2

Many Indian restaurant menus offer a 'traditional' curry sauce. This dish is typically mild-medium and often uses a little cream towards the end of cooking to create a smooth, silky sauce.

1 large skinless, boneless chicken breast fillet (around
   113 g/4 oz weight)
½ teaspoon vegetable oil
½ teaspoon garlic and ginger paste
1 teaspoon tomato purée
1 teaspoon lemon juice
Pinch of salt
½ teaspoon mild Madras curry powder
¼ teaspoon paprika
¼ teaspoon coriander powder
¼ teaspoon cumin powder
¼ teaspoon turmeric powder
½ teaspoon chilli powder
¼ teaspoon salt
½ teaspoon sugar
1 teaspoon dried fenugreek leaves
300 ml/10½ fl oz Basic Curry Sauce (page 40)
3–4 tablespoons vegetable oil
½ small onion, finely chopped
1 teaspoon garlic and ginger paste
2 tablespoons tomato purée, mixed with 4 tablespoons water
1 large handful of chopped fresh coriander
½ tomato, chopped
1–2 tablespoons single cream (optional)
Chopped fresh coriander to garnish

Trim any excess fat from the chicken breast and cut into 5–6 pieces. In a large bowl or food-safe bag, add the vegetable oil, garlic and ginger paste, tomato purée, lemon juice and salt. Mix well and marinade for at least 1 hour, or overnight if possible.

In a small bowl, combine the curry powder, paprika, coriander powder, cumin powder, turmeric, chilli powder, salt, sugar and dried fenugreek. Set aside.

In a small pan, bring the basic curry sauce to boiling point. Stir well, switch off the heat and set aside.

Heat the vegetable oil in a frying pan or wok over a medium heat. Add the chopped onion and garlic and ginger paste. Stir-fry for 2–3 minutes or until the garlic begins to brown.

Add the tomato purée and water mixture. Mix well and stir-fry for 1 minute.

Add the bowl of spices. Stir-fry for 30–40 seconds. Stir and scrape the pan often with a spatula or spoon to ensure the spices do not burn.

Add the chicken pieces and stir-fry for 1–2 minutes or until sealed.

Add around half (150 ml/5 fl oz) of the preheated basic curry sauce. Mix well; increase the heat to high and stir-fry for a further 3–4 minutes.

Add the remaining basic curry sauce and mix well. Add the fresh coriander and chopped fresh tomatoes. Stir-fry for a further 1 minute.

Add the single cream if desired, mix well once more and stir-fry for a further 3–4 minutes or until the sauce reaches the desired consistency.

Ladle the curry into a serving tray and garnish with fresh coriander. Serve with pilau rice and nan bread or chapattis.

CHICKEN/LAMB TIKKA

(INDIAN RESTAURANT STYLE)

Serves 4

This mildly spiced tikka marinade will create deliciously flavoured chunks of meat which will freeze well for up to 3 months in batches of 3–4 pieces and can be used in any of the curry dishes in this book.

6 large skinless, boneless chicken breast fillets (around 113 g/
    4 oz weight per breast) or equivalent weight of boneless
    lamb leg steaks
1½ tablespoons tikka paste (recommended brand: Patak's)
½ tablespoon garlic and ginger paste
4 tablespoons natural yogurt
2 tablespoons vegetable oil
6 tablespoons water
2 tablespoons lemon juice
1 teaspoon mint sauce
1–2 drops of natural red food colour (optional)
½ teaspoon mild Madras curry powder
½ teaspoon coriander powder
¼ teaspoon cumin powder
½ teaspoon garam masala
½ teaspoon turmeric
¼ teaspoon chilli powder
¼ teaspoon cayenne pepper
1 teaspoon dried fenugreek leaves
½ teaspoon salt

Trim any excess fat from the meat and cut each breast into 3–4 large pieces.

In a large bowl, combine the tikka paste, garlic and ginger paste, natural yogurt, vegetable oil, water, lemon juice, mint sauce, natural red food colour (optional), curry powder, coriander powder, cumin powder, garam masala, turmeric, chilli powder, cayenne pepper, dried fenugreek leaves and salt.

Mix thoroughly and add the meat. Marinade for at least 4 hours or overnight if possible.

Preheat the oven to 200°C/400°F/Gas Mark 6.

Arrange the tikka pieces on a wire rack over a roasting tray and bake on the highest oven shelf for 7 minutes.

Turn the tikka pieces and bake for a further 7 minutes.

Turn the tikka pieces once more and bake for a further 5–6 minutes or until just beginning to char. Serve the chicken or lamb tikka pieces as a kebab with Pitta Salad (page 123), or cool and freeze for up to 3 months for use in Indian curry dishes.

CHICKEN TIKKA MASALA

(INDIAN RESTAURANT STYLE)

Serves 1–2

200 ml/7 fl oz Basic Curry Sauce (page 40)
1 tablespoon vegetable oil
4 tablespoons coconut powder
3 tablespoons sugar
4 tablespoons tikka marinade
3–4 pieces of cooked chicken tikka
100 ml/3½ fl oz single cream
1 teaspoon single cream to finish

In a small pot, bring the basic curry sauce to boiling point. Stir well, switch off the heat and set aside.

Heat the vegetable oil in a frying pan or wok over a low-medium heat.

Add the preheated basic curry sauce, coconut powder and sugar. Mix thoroughly, scraping and stirring the pan until the coconut and sugar are fully mixed with the sauce. Increase the heat to high and stir-fry for 1–2 minutes.

Add the tikka marinade and mix well. Add the cooked chicken tikka pieces and continue to fry for a further 2–3 minutes. Slice the tikka pieces in half if desired.

Add the single cream and mix well once again. Stir-fry for a further 3–4 minutes or until the sauce reaches the desired consistency.

Ladle the curry into a serving tray and finish with a teaspoon of single cream. Serve with pilau rice and nan bread or chapattis.

LAMB TIKKA DANSAK

(INDIAN RESTAURANT STYLE)

Serves 1–2

1 teaspoon mild Madras curry powder
½ teaspoon paprika
½ teaspoon coriander powder
½ teaspoon cumin powder
½ teaspoon turmeric powder
1 teaspoon chilli powder
¼ teaspoon salt
1½ tablespoons sugar
300 ml/10½ fl oz Basic Curry Sauce (page 40)
2 tablespoons vegetable oil
2 tablespoons tomato purée, mixed with 4 tablespoons water
5–6 tablespoons cooked plain dal
5–6 pieces of cooked lamb tikka
1 tablespoon lemon juice
1 small handful of chopped fresh coriander

In a small bowl, combine the curry powder, paprika, coriander powder, cumin powder, turmeric, chilli powder, salt and sugar. Set aside.

In a small pan, bring the basic curry sauce to boiling point. Stir well, switch off the heat and set aside.

Heat the vegetable oil in a frying pan or wok over a medium heat. Add the tomato purée and water mixture. Mix well and stir-fry for 30 seconds. Add the bowl of spices. Mix well and stir-fry for 1 minute.

Add around half (150 ml/5 fl oz) of the basic curry sauce. Mix well and stir-fry for 2–3 minutes. Add the dal and remaining basic curry sauce. Increase the heat to high and stir-fry for a further 2 minutes.

Add the cooked lamb tikka pieces. Mix well and cook for a further 2 minutes.

Add the lemon juice and fresh coriander. Mix well and cook for a further 5–6 minutes or until the lamb is heated through and the sauce reaches the desired consistency.

SOUTH INDIAN GARLIC CHILLI CHICKEN TIKKA

(INDIAN RESTAURANT STYLE)

Serves 1–2

This dish is relatively new on UK restaurant menus but is already considered a classic. Many restaurants use a combination of fresh, dried and powdered chilli peppers, while some prefer to rely on only fresh chillies for heat. Whichever method is preferred by your local restaurant, one truth remains; this dish is not for the faint hearted!

1 teaspoon mild Madras curry powder
½ teaspoon paprika
½ teaspoon coriander powder
½ teaspoon cumin powder
½ teaspoon turmeric
2 teaspoons chilli powder
¼ teaspoon salt
2 teaspoons dried fenugreek leaves
2 teaspoons sugar
300 ml/10½ fl oz Basic Curry Sauce (page 40)
3–4 tablespoons vegetable oil
¼ small onion, finely chopped
3 cloves of garlic, finely chopped
3 cloves of garlic, finely sliced
3 green finger chilli peppers, finely sliced (see page 39)
2 tablespoons tomato purée, mixed with 4 tablespoons water
100 g tinned chopped tomatoes (¼ of an average tin)
3–4 pieces of cooked chicken tikka
1 large handful of finely chopped fresh coriander
½ tomato, chopped
Chopped fresh coriander to garnish

In a small bowl, combine the curry powder, paprika, coriander powder, cumin powder, turmeric powder, chilli powder, salt, dried fenugreek leaves and sugar. Set aside.

In a small pan, bring the basic curry sauce to boiling point. Stir well, switch off the heat and set aside.

Heat the vegetable oil in a frying pan or wok over a medium heat. Add the chopped onion and stir-fry for 2–3 minutes.

Add the chopped garlic, sliced garlic and sliced chillies. Stir-fry for a further 2–3 minutes or until the garlic begins to brown.

Add the tomato purée and water mixture and tinned tomatoes. Mix well and stir-fry for 1 minute.

Add the bowl of spices. Stir-fry for 2 minutes. Stir and scrape the pan often with a spatula or spoon to ensure the spices do not burn.

Add around a third (100 ml/3½ fl oz) of the basic curry sauce. Mix well; increase the heat to high and stir-fry for a further 2–3 minutes.

Add another third of the basic curry sauce. Mix well once again, add the cooked chicken tikka pieces and continue to fry for a further 2–3 minutes. Slice the tikka pieces in half if desired.

Add the remaining basic curry sauce. Mix thoroughly and stir-fry for a further 3–4 minutes.

Add the fresh coriander and chopped tomato. Mix well.

Stir-fry for a further 1–2 minutes or until the sauce reaches the desired consistency.

Ladle the curry into a serving tray and garnish with fresh coriander. Serve with turmeric rice and nan bread or chapattis.

CHICKEN TIKKA CHASNI

(INDIAN RESTAURANT STYLE)

Serves 1–2

This curry is very different from anything else on the menu with its sweet and sour flavours and is another modern Indian curry dish thought to have been invented in Scotland!

1 teaspoon mild Madras curry powder
½ teaspoon paprika
½ teaspoon coriander powder
½ teaspoon cumin powder
½ teaspoon turmeric powder
¼ teaspoon chilli powder
Pinch of salt
1 teaspoon dried fenugreek leaves
250 ml/9 fl oz Basic Curry Sauce (page 40)
2 tablespoons vegetable oil
½ small onion, chopped
1 teaspoon garlic and ginger paste
2 tablespoons tomato purée, mixed with 4 tablespoons water
4–5 pieces of cooked chicken tikka
1 tablespoon tomato ketchup
1 tablespoon mango chutney
1 teaspoon mint sauce
1–2 teaspoons lemon juice
1–2 drops of natural red food colour (optional)
1 handful of chopped fresh coriander
75 ml/2½ fl oz single cream
Fresh coriander to garnish

In a small bowl, combine the curry powder, paprika, coriander powder, cumin powder, turmeric, chilli powder, pinch of salt and dried fenugreek leaves. Set aside.

In a small pan, bring the basic curry sauce to boiling point. Stir well, switch off the heat and set aside.

Heat the vegetable oil in a frying pan or wok over a medium heat. Add the chopped onion and garlic and ginger paste. Stir-fry for 2–3 minutes or until the garlic begins to brown.

Add the tomato purée and water mixture. Mix well and stir-fry for 30 seconds.

Add the bowl of spices. Stir-fry for 2 minutes. Stir and scrape the pan often with a spatula or spoon to ensure the spices do not burn.

Add around half (125 ml/4 fl oz) of the basic curry sauce. Mix well; increase the heat to high and stir-fry for a further 1–2 minutes.

Add the cooked chicken tikka pieces and stir-fry for 1 minute. Slice the tikka pieces in half if desired.

Add the tomato ketchup, mango chutney, mint sauce and lemon juice. Mix well and stir-fry for a further 2–3 minutes.

Add the remaining basic curry sauce. Mix well once again and continue to fry for a further 2–3 minutes. Add 1–2 drops of natural red food colour if desired.

Add the chopped coriander and mix thoroughly. Add the single cream. Mix well and continue to cook for a further 3–4 minutes or until the sauce reaches the desired consistency.

Ladle the curry into a serving tray, garnish with fresh coriander and serve with turmeric rice and nan bread or chapattis.

CHICKEN KORMA
(INDIAN RESTAURANT STYLE)

Serves 1–2

This mild, sweet and creamy curry is an ideal introduction to the world of Indian food for those who may be intimidated by the hot spices often associated with curry. Coconut and cream combine to make a mellow sauce which is delicious mopped up with nan bread and chapattis.

1 large skinless, boneless chicken breast fillet (around
    113 g/4 oz weight)
½ teaspoon vegetable oil
½ teaspoon garlic and ginger paste
1 teaspoon tomato purée
1 teaspoon lemon juice
Pinch of salt
250 ml/9 fl oz Basic Curry Sauce (page 40)
1 tablespoon vegetable oil
3 tablespoons coconut powder
3–4 tablespoons sugar
75 ml/2½ fl oz single cream
1 teaspoon single cream to finish

Trim any excess fat from the chicken breast and cut into 5–6 pieces. In a large bowl or food-safe bag, add the vegetable oil, garlic and ginger paste, tomato purée, lemon juice and salt. Mix well and marinade for at least 1 hour or overnight if possible.

In a small pan, bring the basic curry sauce to boiling point. Stir well, switch off the heat and set aside.

Heat the oil in a pan over a medium-high heat. Add the chicken pieces and stir-fry for 1–2 minutes or until sealed.

Add the basic curry sauce, coconut powder and sugar. Mix thoroughly, scraping and stirring the pan until the coconut and sugar are dissolved. Increase the heat to high and stir-fry for 2–3 minutes.

Add the single cream, mix thoroughly and cook for a further 5–6 minutes or until the sauce reaches the desired consistency.

Ladle the curry into a serving tray and finish with a teaspoon of single cream. Serve with turmeric rice and nan bread or chapattis.

LAMB TIKKA JALFREZI

(INDIAN RESTAURANT STYLE)

Serves 1–2

1 teaspoon mild Madras curry powder
½ teaspoon paprika
½ teaspoon coriander powder
½ teaspoon cumin powder
½ teaspoon turmeric powder
Pinch of chilli powder
¼ teaspoon salt
1 teaspoon dried fenugreek leaves
300 ml/10½ fl oz Basic Curry Sauce (page 40)
2 tablespoons vegetable oil
1 small onion, chopped
½ green pepper, sliced
½ red pepper, sliced
2 green ginger chilli peppers, finely sliced (see page 39)
1 teaspoon garlic and ginger paste
2 cloves of garlic, finely sliced
2 tablespoons tomato purée, mixed with 4 tablespoons water
3–4 pieces of cooked lamb tikka
1 handful of chopped fresh coriander
1 tomato, cut into 8 pieces
Fresh coriander to garnish

In a small bowl, combine the curry powder, paprika, coriander powder, cumin powder, turmeric, chilli powder, salt and dried fenugreek leaves. Set aside.

In a small pan, bring the basic curry sauce to boiling point. Stir well, switch off the heat and set aside.

Heat the vegetable oil in a frying pan or wok over a medium heat. Add the chopped onion and sliced peppers. Stir-fry for 5–6 minutes.

Add the sliced chilli peppers, garlic and ginger paste and finely sliced garlic cloves. Stir-fry for 2–3 minutes or until the garlic begins to brown.

Add the tomato purée and water mixture. Mix well and stir-fry for 30 seconds.

Add the bowl of spices. Stir-fry for 2 minutes. Stir and scrape the pan often with a spatula or spoon to ensure the spices do not burn.

Add around half (150 ml/5 fl oz) of the basic curry sauce. Mix well; increase the heat to high and stir-fry for a further 1–2 minutes.

Add the cooked lamb tikka pieces and stir-fry for 1 minute. Slice the tikka pieces in half if desired.

Add the remaining basic curry sauce. Mix thoroughly and stir-fry for a further 3–4 minutes.

Add the fresh coriander and chopped tomato. Mix well and stir-fry for a further 1–2 minutes or until the sauce reaches the desired consistency.

Ladle the curry into a serving tray, garnish with fresh coriander and serve with turmeric rice and nan bread or chapattis.

MIXED VEGETABLE CURRY

(INDIAN RESTAURANT STYLE)

Serves 1–2

Almost any selection of vegetables will work well with this dish. Frozen vegetables can be cooked in the microwave to hurry things along if desired. Allow the cooked vegetables to cool completely before use in the final dish.

½ teaspoon mild Madras curry powder
¼ teaspoon paprika
¼ teaspoon coriander powder
¼ teaspoon cumin powder
¼ teaspoon turmeric
1 teaspoon chilli powder
¼ teaspoon salt
1 teaspoon dried fenugreek leaves
1 large potato, peeled and cubed
2–3 large cauliflower florets, chopped
2 tablespoons frozen peas
300 ml/10½ fl oz Basic Curry Sauce (page 40)
3 tablespoons vegetable oil
1 teaspoon garlic and ginger paste
½ small onion, finely chopped
2 cloves of garlic, finely chopped
2 tablespoons tomato purée, mixed with 4 tablespoons water
1 large handful of chopped fresh coriander
1 tomato, chopped
Fresh coriander to garnish

In a bowl, combine the curry powder, paprika, coriander powder, cumin powder, turmeric, chilli powder, salt and dried fenugreek leaves. Set aside.

Fill a large pan with water and bring to the boil. Add the cubed potato, chopped cauliflower and frozen peas to the pan and simmer for 5 minutes. Drain and rinse the vegetables with cold water. Drain once more and set aside.

In a small pan, bring the basic curry sauce to boiling point. Stir well, switch off the heat and set aside.

Heat the vegetable oil in a frying pan or wok over a low heat. Add the garlic and ginger paste, chopped onion and garlic. Stir-fry for 2 minutes.

Add the tomato purée and water mixture and stir well. Stir-fry for 30 seconds.

Add the bowl of spices. Stir and scrape the pan often with a spatula or spoon to ensure the spices do not burn. Stir-fry for a further 2 minutes.

Add around half (150 ml/5 fl oz) of the basic curry sauce. Stir-fry for 1 minute.

Add the prepared vegetables, increase the heat to medium-high and stir-fry for a further 1–2 minutes.

Add the remaining basic curry sauce. Increase the heat to high and mix thoroughly. Stir-fry for a further 2–3 minutes.

Add the chopped coriander and chopped fresh tomato. Mix well and stir-fry for a further 2 minutes or until the vegetables are heated through and the sauce reaches the desired consistency.

Ladle the curry into a serving tray and garnish with fresh coriander. Serve with turmeric rice and chapattis.

TARKA DAL

(INDIAN RESTAURANT STYLE)

Serves 1–2

This basic dal is very nutritious and can be flavoured with any number of different spices or 'tarka'. Plain dal can be prepared in advance, reheated and finished with the tarka just before serving, making it an extremely convenient dish. Plain dal can also be reserved for use in dansak style Indian curry dishes.

60 g/2 oz red lentils (uncooked weight)
500 ml/18 fl oz water
½ onion, thinly sliced
½ teaspoon turmeric
¼ teaspoon salt
3 tablespoons vegetable oil
½ teaspoon mustard seeds
¼ teaspoon cumin seeds
2 whole dried chilli peppers
3–4 curry leaves
Pinch of chilli powder
2 teaspoons garlic and ginger paste
1 tomato, finely chopped
1 small handful of chopped fresh coriander

Wash the lentils thoroughly in cold water until the water runs clear.

In a pan, combine the red lentils, water, sliced onion and turmeric. Bring back to the boil, skimming off any froth from the middle of the pan.

Reduce the heat to a simmer and cook the lentils for 40–45 minutes or until soft, stirring occasionally. Add more water if the lentils dry out too quickly and stir them often to ensure they do not begin to catch on the bottom of the pan.

When the lentils are soft, add the salt and use a potato masher to mash the lentils a little.

At this stage, the plain dal can be refrigerated or frozen for future use. The cooked dal freezes well for up to 1 month. Plain Dal can also be stored in 5–6 tablespoon batches for use in dansak style curry dishes such as Lamb Tikka Dansak (page 49).

To finish the tarka dal, heat the vegetable oil in a separate small pan over a medium heat.

Add the mustard seeds, cumin seeds, dried chilli peppers, curry leaves, chilli powder and garlic and ginger paste. Stir-fry for 2–3 minutes.

Pour the fried mixture into the cooked dal and mix well.

Add the chopped tomato and fresh coriander. Mix well once more and simmer on a low heat for 1–2 minutes.

Ladle the dal into a serving tray and garnish with fresh coriander. Serve with turmeric rice and chapattis.

6

CHINESE MAIN MEALS

The most important item of equipment required in Chinese cooking is undoubtedly the wok. A good quality, well seasoned wok will last a lifetime and is a worthy investment. Any large frying pan will provide an excellent substitute, provided it is large enough to enable quick stirring of the ingredients. Regardless of the pan used, a high heat is essential when the final cooking process begins.

As with the Indian curry dishes in this book, Chinese stir-fry cooking requires preparation in order to ensure that the final cooking of the meal happens quickly and easily. By preparing the ingredients in advance, your attention can remain focused on the wok and its ingredients, allowing you to ensure the pan is stirred constantly to prevent burning over a high heat.

People often comment on the silky and tender meat used in Chinese stir-fry dishes. This is achieved using a cornflour marinade similar to the one described in this chapter and takes no time at all to prepare. Unlike other marinades which may need to be left overnight, this simple technique works in minutes. Almost all of the meats used in Chinese restaurant dishes begin life in this marinade which protects the meat and seals the juices inside while cooking.

Chinese cooking ingredients can be purchased from any good supermarket; however it's well worth seeking out a large Chinese supermarket if there is one in your area, where you're sure to find a huge range of Chinese and other Far Eastern ingredients.

The recipes included in this chapter are based around the dishes typically offered by Chinese takeaways and restaurants. Stir-fry cooking is an ideal way to combine various meats and vegetables, however, so do experiment with other ingredients. Chow mein and fried rice dishes are particularly versatile and work extremely well with any sliced vegetables.

BEEF CHOW MEIN

(CHINESE TAKEAWAY STYLE)

Serves 1–2

1 x 200 g/7 oz sirloin steak
1 teaspoon soy sauce (recommended brand: Kikkoman)
½ teaspoon garlic powder
¼ teaspoon ginger powder
1 tablespoon vegetable oil
1 teaspoon cornflour
1 tablespoon oyster sauce
1 tablespoon soy sauce (recommended brand: Kikkoman)
50 ml/2 fl oz chicken stock
½ teaspoon cornflour
1 nest of egg noodles
1 tablespoon toasted sesame oil
1 clove of garlic, finely chopped
1 x 2.5 cm/1 inch piece of ginger, finely chopped
1 onion, finely sliced
50 g/2 oz bean sprouts
¼ teaspoon black pepper

Trim any excess fat from the sirloin steak and cut into small, thin strips. Add the soy sauce, garlic powder, ginger powder and vegetable oil. Mix well and marinade for 5 minutes. Add the cornflour and mix well once again. Leave to rest for 10 minutes.

In a small bowl, combine the oyster sauce, soy sauce, chicken stock and cornflour. Mix thoroughly and set aside.

Drop the egg noodles into boiling water and simmer for 2–3 minutes, stirring well to separate the noodles. Rinse thoroughly under cold water, drain and toss with toasted sesame oil, then set aside.

Heat a wok or frying pan to a high heat. Add a little vegetable oil. Drop the steak slices into the pan and leave for 30 seconds to seal. Stir fry the beef for around 3–4 minutes or until just cooked through. Remove and set aside.

Add the chopped garlic and ginger, sliced onion and bean sprouts to the pan and stir-fry for 2–3 minutes. Add the noodles and stir-fry for a further 1 minute.

Return the beef to the pan and pour in the prepared sauce. Mix thoroughly and cook for a further 1–2 minutes or until the sauce just begins to thicken. Season with the black pepper and serve with prawn crackers.

CHILLI CHICKEN CHOW MEIN

(CHINESE TAKEAWAY STYLE)

Serves 1–2

1 large skinless, boneless chicken breast fillet (around
  113 g/4 oz weight)
1 teaspoon soy sauce (recommended brand: Kikkoman)
½ teaspoon garlic powder
¼ teaspoon ginger powder
¼ teaspoon Chinese five-spice powder
1 tablespoon vegetable oil
1 teaspoon cornflour
2 tablespoons sweet chilli sauce
1 tablespoon tomato ketchup (recommended brand: Heinz)
1 teaspoon soy sauce (recommended brand: Kikkoman)
50 ml/2 fl oz water
1 nest of egg noodles
1 tablespoon toasted sesame oil
1 clove of garlic, finely chopped
1 x 2.5 cm/1 inch piece of ginger, finely chopped
1 onion, finely sliced
½ red pepper, finely sliced
½ green pepper, finely sliced
1 carrot, grated
1 small handful of shredded cabbage or Chinese leaves

Trim any excess fat from the chicken breast and cut into small, thin strips. Add the soy sauce, garlic powder, ginger powder, Chinese five-spice and vegetable oil. Mix well and marinade for 5 minutes. Add 1 teaspoon of cornflour and mix well again.

In a small bowl, combine the sweet chilli sauce, tomato ketchup, soy sauce and water. Mix well and set aside.

Drop the egg noodles into boiling water and simmer for 2–3 minutes, stirring well to separate the noodles. Rinse thoroughly under cold water, drain and toss with toasted sesame oil, then set aside.

Heat a wok or frying pan to a high heat. Add a little vegetable oil. Drop the chicken pieces into the pan and leave for 30 seconds to seal. Stir fry the chicken for around 3–4 minutes or until just cooked through. Remove and set aside.

Add the chopped garlic and ginger, sliced onion, red pepper, green pepper, carrot and shredded cabbage or Chinese leaves to the pan and stir-fry for 3–4 minutes.

Add the egg noodles and stir-fry for a further 1 minute.

Return the chicken to the pan and pour in the prepared chilli sauce. Mix well and cook for a further 1–2 minutes or until the sauce just begins to thicken. Serve with prawn crackers.

SZECHUAN CHICKEN

(Chinese Takeaway Style)

Serves 1–2

Using freshly squeezed apple juice will produce a far superior result in this dish. You don't have to juice the apples yourself, but choosing a fresh brand from your supermarket over a concentrated juice will prove very worthwhile.

2 tablespoons pure apple juice
½ teaspoon Worcester sauce
1 teaspoon Tabasco sauce
1 tablespoon toasted sesame oil
½ tablespoon soy sauce (recommended brand: Kikkoman)
1 tablespoon brown sugar
1 dried chilli pepper, crushed
Pinch of cayenne pepper
1 x 2.5 cm/1 inch piece of ginger, finely chopped
2 tablespoons water
1 large skinless, boneless chicken breast fillet (around
    113 g/4 oz weight)
1 teaspoon soy sauce (recommended brand: Kikkoman)
½ teaspoon garlic powder
1 tablespoon vegetable oil
1 teaspoon cornflour
1 clove of garlic, finely chopped
1 x 2.5 cm/1 inch piece of ginger, finely chopped
1 green pepper, chopped
1 onion, chopped

In a bowl, combine the apple juice, Worcester sauce, Tabasco sauce, sesame oil, soy sauce, brown sugar, dried chilli, cayenne pepper, finely chopped ginger and water. Mix thoroughly and set aside.

Trim any excess fat from the chicken breast and cut into small bite sized pieces. Add the soy sauce, garlic powder and vegetable oil. Mix well and marinade for 5 minutes. Add 1 teaspoon of cornflour and mix well again.

Heat a wok or frying pan to a high heat. Add a little vegetable oil. Drop the chicken pieces into the pan and leave for 30 seconds to seal. Stir fry the chicken for around 3–4 minutes or until just cooked through. Remove and set aside.

Add the chopped garlic and ginger, green pepper and onion to the pan and stir-fry for 2–3 minutes.

Return the chicken to the pan and pour in the prepared Szechuan sauce. Mix well and cook for a further 1–2 minutes or until the sauce just begins to thicken. Serve with fried rice and prawn crackers.

SKEWERED CHICKEN SATAY

(CHINESE TAKEAWAY STYLE)

Serves 1–2

1 tablespoon vegetable oil
½ small onion, finely chopped
1 teaspoon mild Madras curry powder
3 tablespoons peanut butter
2 teaspoons soy sauce
200 ml/7 fl oz coconut milk
75 ml/2½ fl oz water
1 tablespoon brown sugar
Pinch of dried chilli flakes
4 wooden skewers
1 large skinless, boneless chicken breast fillet (around
    113 g/4 oz weight)
1 teaspoon soy sauce (recommended brand: Kikkoman)
½ teaspoon garlic powder
¼ teaspoon ginger powder
1 tablespoon vegetable oil
1 teaspoon cornflour

In a small saucepan or frying pan, heat the vegetable oil over a low-medium heat. Add the chopped onion and stir fry for 1–2 minutes until just beginning to soften.

Add the curry powder and stir-fry for 1 minute.

Add the peanut butter and stir-fry for another minute until beginning to melt.

Add the soy sauce, coconut milk, water, brown sugar and dried chilli flakes. Bring to the boil then simmer on a low heat until the sauce is combined and the desired consistency is reached. Remove from the heat and set aside. The sauce will thicken upon cooling and can be reheated when needed, adding a little water if necessary.

Soak the wooden skewers in cold water for 30 minutes to prevent them from burning.

Trim any excess fat from the chicken breast and cut into 6–8 long, thin strips. Add the soy sauce, garlic powder, ginger powder and vegetable oil. Mix well and marinade for 5 minutes. Add 1 teaspoon of cornflour and mix well again.

Ribbon the chicken strips onto the soaked wooden skewers, piercing each piece of chicken several times. Each skewer should comfortably hold 2 strips of chicken.

Grill the skewered chicken on a high heat for around 2 minutes per side, or until the chicken is cooked through and just beginning to char. The skewered chicken pieces also cook very well on a double-plated health grill.

Remove the cooked chicken skewers and arrange on a serving plate. Drizzle with the prepared satay sauce and serve with fried rice.

SHREDDED CRISPY CHICKEN

(CHINESE TAKEAWAY STYLE)

Serves 1–2

3 tablespoons sweet chilli sauce
1 teaspoon honey
¼ teaspoon garlic powder
1 tablespoon water
1 large skinless, boneless chicken breast fillet (around
    113 g/4 oz weight)
1 teaspoon soy sauce (recommended brand: Kikkoman)
½ teaspoon garlic powder
¼ teaspoon ginger powder
2 teaspoons vegetable oil
60 g/2 oz cornflour
Oil for deep frying

In a small bowl, combine the sweet chilli sauce, honey, garlic powder and water. Mix well and set aside.

Trim any excess fat from the chicken breast and cut into small bite sized pieces. Add the soy sauce, garlic powder, ginger powder and vegetable oil. Mix well and rest for 5 minutes.

Heat the oil to a medium-high heat. Dip the chicken pieces into the cornflour until fully coated, and then drop carefully into the hot oil.

Fry the chicken pieces for 5–6 minutes or until the chicken is cooked through and the coating becomes crispy.

Drain the chicken pieces of any excess oil and immediately mix with the prepared sauce.

Continue to stir the sauce through the chicken for 1 minute until well combined. Serve with fried rice and prawn crackers.

CHAR SIU (CHINESE ROAST PORK)

(CHINESE TAKEAWAY STYLE)

Serves 3–4

If desired, the marinated pork fillet may be sliced into long, thin strips and grilled on skewers to create individual char siu kebabs.

1 tablespoon honey
1 tablespoon rice wine
3–4 tablespoons water
2 teaspoons soy sauce (recommended brand: Kikkoman)
3 tablespoons hoisin or barbecue sauce
2 tablespoons tomato ketchup
1 teaspoon toasted sesame oil
¼ teaspoon Chinese five-spice powder
½ teaspoon garlic powder
¼ teaspoon ginger powder
Roughly 500 g/1.1 lb pork fillet

In a bowl, combine the honey, rice wine, water, soy sauce, hoisin sauce, tomato ketchup, toasted sesame oil, Chinese five-spice, garlic powder and ginger powder.

Add the pork fillet and rub the marinade thoroughly into the meat. Marinade for at least 4 hours or overnight if possible, turning the pork fillet occasionally.

Preheat the oven to 200°C/400°F/Gas Mark 6. Pour 100 ml/3½ fl oz of water into a roasting tray and place the marinated pork fillet on a rack above the tray. Place into the hot oven and roast for 35–40 minutes or until cooked through. When the char siu is cooked, remove from the oven and rest for 4–5 minutes.

To create a sauce or glaze for the dish, any leftover marinade can be brought to the boil and simmered for 2–3 minutes. Pour the simmering marinade over the sliced, cooked char siu and serve with fried rice.

CHICKEN BALLS WITH
SWEET AND SOUR SAUCE

(CHINESE TAKEAWAY STYLE)

Serves 1–2

60 ml/2 fl oz tomato ketchup
20 ml/1 fl oz white vinegar
70 ml/2½ fl oz water
¼ teaspoon soy sauce
70 g/2½ oz white sugar
35 g/1¼ oz brown sugar
1½ tablespoons cornflour
30 ml/1½ fl oz water
120 g/4 oz plain flour
120 g/4 oz cornflour
½ tablespoon baking powder
½ tablespoon bicarbonate of soda
½ tablespoon sugar
220 ml/8 fl oz water
1 large skinless, boneless chicken breast fillet (around
    113 g/4 oz weight)
Oil for deep frying

In a small pan, combine the tomato ketchup, white vinegar, water, soy sauce, white sugar and brown sugar. On a low-medium heat, bring the mixture to boiling point, stirring frequently. Once the mixture is boiling, allow to simmer for 1–2 minutes.

In a separate bowl, combine 1½ tablespoons of cornflour and 30 ml/1½ fl oz of water. Mix thoroughly and add to the simmering pan. Continue stirring frequently and simmer for a further 2–3 minutes. Remove the pan from the heat and pour the sweet and sour sauce into a serving bowl or tub. Set aside.

In a large bowl, combine the plain flour, cornflour, baking powder, bicarbonate of soda, sugar and water. Whisk thoroughly until a smooth batter is formed.

Trim any excess fat from the chicken breast and cut into 7–8 pieces.

Preheat oil for deep frying to medium-high. Dip the chicken pieces into the batter and then drop carefully into the hot oil. Fry for 5–6 minutes or until the batter is golden and the chicken balls are cooked through.

Remove the chicken balls from the pan and drain off any excess oil. Serve with the prepared sweet and sour sauce, fried rice and prawn crackers.

GRIDDLED SIRLOIN STEAK

(Chinese Takeaway Style)

Serves 1

Chinese Gravy:
1 teaspoon vegetable oil
1 clove of garlic, finely chopped
1 x 2.5 cm/1 inch piece of ginger, finely chopped
½ onion, finely chopped
5–6 button mushrooms, sliced
2 tablespoons of beef gravy powder
280 ml/½ pint water
1 tablespoon soy sauce
¼ teaspoon Chinese five-spice powder
1 teaspoon sugar
½ onion, finely sliced

1 x 200 g/7 oz sirloin steak
1 tablespoon vegetable oil
¼ teaspoon salt
¼ teaspoon black pepper

Heat 1 teaspoon of vegetable oil in a pan on a low heat. Add the sliced garlic and ginger, stir fry for 30 seconds and add the chopped onion.

Stir fry the garlic, ginger and chopped onion for 2–3 minutes on a low heat. Add the mushrooms and continue to stir fry for another 3–4 minutes.

Combine the gravy powder and water in a bowl and add to the pan. Turn the heat up to high and add the soy sauce, Chinese five-spice and sugar. Bring to the boil and simmer on a medium heat for 4–5 minutes until the gravy reaches the desired consistency. Add more water if necessary. Mix the finely sliced onion through the finished gravy.

Heat a dry griddle pan to a high heat. Rub the vegetable oil, salt and black pepper into the steak. Place the steak onto the hot griddle and cook for 2–3 minutes per side, turning only once, or until cooked to preferred taste. Remove and set aside to rest for 3–4 minutes.

7

PIZZA AND PASTA

When it comes to takeaway food, pizza is one of the most popular options, particularly amongst those who might be hungry for leftovers the following day! With a good pizza base and sauce, any number of topping combinations can be experimented with, making it a great option for those who like variety. When you make your own pizza at home, you also have the added bonus of not paying huge sums of money for each chosen topping!

Takeaway restaurants have one very important advantage over home cooks when it comes to cooking pizza, namely the pizza oven itself. Dedicated pizza ovens can reach temperatures far in excess of those possible in a home oven, in some cases upwards of 500° Celsius. This makes replicating takeaway pizza at home a difficult task, though not an impossible one. The cooking instructions listed in the recipes in this chapter will offer a good starting point; but do experiment. With some trial and error, you'll soon find the best cooking method to suit your needs and your oven.

Home pizza maker ovens are now widely available, many of which allow cooking of both pan and stone bake pizzas. These ovens still fall a little short when compared to professional pizza ovens, but will almost certainly offer significantly better results than most conventional home ovens. If you're serious about your pizza, you'll probably be interested in purchasing one of these ovens, or at the very least a pizza stone for use in your home oven. Many people believe that a pizza stone preheated over a long time makes the best home pizzas. If a stone bake base is not desired, a pizza stone can still be very useful in conducting heat to the pizza. To use this method, preheat the pizza stone as normal and place the pizza pan on top to cook.

When topping your pizza, it's important to add additional toppings after the cheese has been added. If vegetables or meat are placed underneath the cheese, moisture will be trapped and the base of your pizza will become soggy. Less is definitely more where pizza toppings are concerned, so try to avoid the temptation to overload your pizza. By keeping the toppings to a minimum, your pizza base will have room to cook properly and offer a crispy, chewy crust.

Although you may by now have been tempted to throw your takeaway menus in the recycle bin, they can still prove very useful at this stage in suggesting topping combinations for your pizza!

Also included in this chapter are two classic pasta dishes, Spaghetti Bolognese and Macaroni Cheese. The third pasta dish, Garlic Cream Fettuccine, is perhaps the most luxurious pasta dish imaginable, combining bacon, cream and cheese for a deliciously smooth dish.

THIN CRUST PIZZA BASE

(ITALIAN RESTAURANT STYLE)

Makes 2 Pizza Bases

230 g/8 oz strong white bread flour
1 x 7 g packet of active dried yeast
1 teaspoon sugar
½ teaspoon salt
1 tablespoon olive oil
Around 120 ml/4 fl oz water

In a large bowl, combine the bread flour, dried yeast and sugar. Mix well. Add the salt and mix again.

Add the olive oil to the bowl and slowly add the water until the dough comes together.

Flour a work surface and pour the dough out. Knead thoroughly for 3–4 minutes until the dough becomes smooth. Shape the dough into a ball.

Rub the bowl with a little olive oil. Return the dough to the bowl and cover with a wet cloth or oiled cling film. Set aside for around 1 hour until doubled in size.

Knock the air out of the risen dough, divide into two pieces and knead for a further 1 minute. Shape the dough into a ball once again.

The dough is now ready for use, or can be frozen for up to 1 month.

ITALIAN PIZZA SAUCE
(ITALIAN RESTAURANT STYLE)

Makes enough sauce for 2–3 Pizzas

This sauce can also be made with fresh basil if available.

2 tablespoons olive oil
1 clove of garlic
1 x 400g tin of plum tomatoes
2 teaspoons dried basil or dried Italian herbs
1 teaspoon sugar
¼ teaspoon salt
Pinch of black pepper

In a small saucepan or frying pan, heat the olive oil over a low heat. Slice the garlic and add to the pan. Stir-fry the garlic for 1 minute. Add the tinned plum tomatoes, dried basil, sugar, salt and black pepper.

Increase the heat and bring the pan to boiling point. Reduce to a simmer and cook for 15–20 minutes. Remove the sauce from the heat and set aside to cool for a few minutes.

Using a food processor or hand blender, process the sauce until it becomes completely smooth. Allow to cool completely and store in the refrigerator for up to 3 days.

INSTANT PIZZA SAUCE

(KEBAB SHOP STYLE)

Makes enough sauce for 1 Pizza

3 tablespoons tomato purée
1 tablespoon olive oil
¼ teaspoon garlic powder
Pinch of onion powder
1 teaspoon dried Italian herbs
Pinch of cayenne pepper
¼ teaspoon salt
Pinch of black pepper
5–6 tablespoons water

In a bowl, combine the tomato purée, olive oil, garlic powder, onion powder, Italian herbs, cayenne pepper, salt and pepper. Add water a little at a time, mixing thoroughly until the sauce reaches the desired consistency.

Allow the sauce to rest at room temperature for 10 minutes before use.

MARGHERITA PIZZA

(ITALIAN RESTAURANT STYLE)

Serves 1–2

The classic pizza topped simply with sauce, mozzarella cheese and fresh tomato slices.

1 prepared 10 inch/25 cm pizza base
2–3 tablespoons Pizza Sauce (page 80)
100 g/3½ oz grated mozzarella cheese
1 tomato, sliced
1 tablespoon olive oil
Pinch of black pepper (optional)

To prepare the pizza base, roll the dough out on a floured surface using hands or a rolling pin and place on a well floured board.

Top the pizza with sauce, spreading the sauce thinly over the pizza base.

Add the mozzarella cheese and sliced tomato. Drizzle 1 tablespoon of olive oil over the topped pizza.

Place a baking tray or pizza stone on the top shelf of the oven. Preheat the oven to 240°C/475°F/Gas Mark 9.

Place the pizza carefully onto the hot baking tray or pizza stone. Bake the pizza for 12–15 minutes or until the base is crispy and the cheese is golden.

Remove the pizza from the oven and garnish with black pepper if desired.

TEXAS STYLE BARBECUE PIZZA

(AMERICAN FAST-FOOD STYLE)

Serves 1–2

1 prepared 10 inch/25 cm pizza base
1–2 tablespoons Pizza Sauce (page 80)
1 tablespoon barbecue sauce
100 g/3½ oz mozzarella cheese, grated
¼ green pepper, sliced
¼ red onion, sliced
7–8 pepperoni slices

To prepare the pizza base, roll the dough out on a floured surface using hands or a rolling pin and place on a well floured board.

Spread the sauces thinly over the pizza base. Add the pizza sauce first, followed by the barbecue sauce.

Add the mozzarella cheese, sliced green pepper, sliced red onion and pepperoni.

Place a baking tray or pizza stone on the top shelf of the oven. Preheat the oven to 240°C/475°F/Gas Mark 9.

Place the pizza carefully onto the hot baking tray or pizza stone. Bake the pizza for 12–15 minutes or until the base is crispy and the cheese is golden.

Remove the pizza from the oven and garnish with black pepper if desired.

VEGETARIAN STUFFED CRUST PIZZA

(American Fast-Food Style)

Serves 1–2

String cheese is often sold as 'snacking cheese' in supermarkets and is ideal for stuffed crust pizzas. Any mild, solid cheese will work well, however, sliced into small thin strips. The vegetables may be stir-fried for 2–3 minutes and cooled before adding to the pizza if desired, however this is not essential.

1 prepared 10 inch/25 cm pizza base
2–3 strips of string cheese
1–2 tablespoons Pizza Sauce (page 80)
100 g/3½ oz mozzarella cheese, grated
¼ green pepper, sliced
¼ red onion, sliced
1 tomato, sliced
2 button mushrooms, thinly sliced
1–2 tablespoons sweetcorn (tinned or frozen)

To prepare the pizza base, roll the dough out on a floured surface using hands or a rolling pin and place on a well floured board.

Place the strips of string cheese near the edges of the pizza base and fold the dough over to seal.

Spread the sauce thinly over the pizza base.

Add the mozzarella cheese, sliced green pepper, sliced red onion, tomato, mushrooms and sweetcorn.

Place a baking tray or pizza stone on the top shelf of the oven. Preheat the oven to 240°C/475°F/Gas Mark 9.

Place the pizza carefully onto the hot baking tray or pizza stone. Bake the pizza for 12–15 minutes or until the base is crispy and the cheese is golden.

Remove the pizza from the oven and garnish with black pepper if desired.

NAN BREAD PEPPERONI PIZZA

(KEBAB SHOP STYLE)

Serves 1

Using homemade or even shop bought nan bread as a pizza base can produce outstanding results, particularly if the nan bread has been cooked in a tandoor oven.

1 nan bread
2 tablespoons Pizza Sauce (page 81)
75 g/3 oz grated mozzarella cheese
5–6 slices of pepperoni
Pinch of black pepper

Preheat a baking tray or pizza stone in the oven to 220°C/425°F/Gas Mark 7.

Spread the instant pizza sauce over the nan bread and add the mozzarella cheese. Top with the pepperoni slices.

Place onto the hot baking tray or pizza stone and cook for 12–15 minutes or until the cheese is golden. Remove the pizza from the oven and garnish with black pepper.

DONER AND SPICED ONIONS CALZONE

(KEBAB SHOP STYLE)

Serves 1–2

Any good pizza topping will double up as an excellent calzone filling.

1 prepared 10 inch/25 cm pizza base
2–3 tablespoons Pizza Sauce (page 81)
100 g/3½ oz mozzarella cheese, grated
10–12 thin slices of cooked lamb doner
2 tablespoons spiced onions

Preheat a baking tray or pizza stone in the oven to 220°C/425°F/Gas Mark 7.

Spread the pizza sauce onto the pizza base.

Add the mozzarella cheese, lamb doner slices and spiced onions over one half of the pizza base. Fold the dough over the filling and press down at the edges to form a seal.

Place onto the hot baking tray or pizza stone and cook for around 15 minutes or until golden.

MACARONI CHEESE
(ITALIAN RESTAURANT STYLE)

Serves 1–2

2 litres/3½ pints water
Pinch of salt
120 g/4 oz of macaroni pasta (dry weight)
75 g/3 oz mild or medium Cheddar cheese, grated
1 tablespoon butter
1 tablespoon plain flour
200 ml/7 fl oz milk
Pinch of salt
¼ teaspoon black pepper
Extra grated cheese for topping (optional)

Add the water to a large pan, add a pinch of salt and bring to the boil. Add the macaroni and allow the pan to return to boiling. Stir the pasta once only to prevent it from sticking. Simmer for 7–8 minutes or until the pasta is just cooked.

In a separate small pot, combine the grated cheese, butter, plain flour, milk, salt and pepper over a low heat. Stir frequently until the sauce becomes smooth and just begins to thicken.

Drain the cooked macaroni and return it to the pan with the cheese sauce. Mix well.

Pour the macaroni and sauce into an oven proof dish. The macaroni cheese can be served immediately, or topped with extra grated cheese and placed into a hot oven or under a hot grill for a few minutes to create a crispy cheese topping.

Serve with garlic bread.

SPAGHETTI BOLOGNESE

(ITALIAN RESTAURANT STYLE)

Serves 4

This Bolognese recipe will easily serve four. Leftovers freeze extremely well for up to 3 months.

1 green pepper
1 x 400 g tin of chopped tomatoes
50 ml/2 fl oz water
½ teaspoon sugar
½ teaspoon paprika
½ teaspoon salt
¼ teaspoon black pepper
1 tablespoon olive oil
500 g/1.1 lb beef mince
1 teaspoon tomato purée
2 teaspoons Worcester sauce
75 g/3 oz spaghetti (uncooked weight) per person to serve
½ teaspoon butter
Grated cheese

In a blender, add the green pepper, chopped tomatoes, water, sugar, paprika, salt and pepper. Blitz well and set aside.

In a large saucepan, heat the olive oil over a medium heat. Add the beef mince and cook for 3–4 minutes. Use a fork to break the mince up as it browns.

Drain off any excess fat from the pan. Return to the heat and add the tomato purée and Worcester sauce. Cook for a further 1–2 minutes, stirring occasionally.

Add the blended ingredients and bring the pan to a boil over a high heat. Reduce the heat to low, place a lid on top and simmer for 1 hour. Stir the Bolognese occasionally; adding a little boiling water or blended tinned tomatoes if the mixture begins to get too dry.

Bring a large pan of water to the boil. Add the spaghetti and stir once. Allow the spaghetti to simmer over a medium-high heat for 5–6 minutes or until just cooked.

Drain the spaghetti and mix well with 2–3 tablespoons of the Bolognese. Add a little butter and grated cheese and mix thoroughly. Serve with garlic bread.

GARLIC CREAM FETTUCCINE WITH BACON AND MUSHROOMS

(ITALIAN RESTAURANT STYLE)

Serves 1–2

This pasta dish is full of indulgence with cream, Parmesan cheese and bacon.

1 teaspoon olive oil
4 slices of smoked bacon, cut into thin strips
3 large chestnut mushrooms, thinly sliced
1 large clove of garlic, finely chopped
½ small onion, finely chopped
1 teaspoon butter
75 ml/2½ fl oz double cream
75 ml/2½ fl oz semi-skimmed milk, mixed with ¾ teaspoon cornflour
1 tablespoon grated Parmesan cheese
Pinch of salt
Pinch of black pepper
100 g/3½ oz fettuccine pasta (uncooked weight)

Heat the oil in a large frying pan over a medium heat. Add the bacon and mushrooms and stir-fry for 6–7 minutes.

Add the chopped garlic and chopped onion. Stir-fry for a further 1 minute.

Add the butter, double cream, semi-skimmed milk and Parmesan cheese. Add salt and pepper and stir thoroughly. Cook for a further 3–4 minutes or until the sauce just starts to thicken.

Fill a large pan with water and bring to the boil. Add a pinch of salt and the fettuccine pasta. Stir once and simmer for 5–6 minutes or until the pasta is just cooked.

Drain the pasta through a sieve, reserving a little of the water. Add the pasta and remaining water to the frying pan and stir well until completely coated in the cream sauce.

Serve with garlic bread.

8

SIDES, SALADS AND SAUCES

Many takeaway restaurants offer excellent value for money, but adding more variety to your meal can quickly increase the cost. Although a main meal may only cost a few pounds, the price is quickly driven up if you add salads or side dishes as accompaniments.

Variety is the spice of life, however, and so it's vital to have a good selection of flavours and dishes to choose from. Thankfully when you prepare these dishes at home, the prices won't increase quite as quickly as they might have from your favourite restaurant, leaving you free to try a little of everything!

PRAWN COCKTAIL

(KEBAB SHOP STYLE)

Serves 1

1 little gem lettuce
100 g/3½ oz cooked, peeled prawns
Pinch of salt
Pinch of black pepper
2 tablespoons mayonnaise
4 teaspoons tomato ketchup
1 teaspoon Worcester sauce
1 teaspoon horseradish
Dash of Tabasco sauce
1 tablespoon lemon juice
Pinch of salt
Pinch of black pepper
Pinch of paprika powder

Line the inside of a glass with the lettuce leaves. Season the prawns with a little salt and pepper and add them to the bowl on top of the lettuce.

In a separate bowl, combine the mayonnaise, ketchup, Worcester sauce, horseradish, Tabasco and lemon juice. Add salt and pepper to taste.

Spoon the sauce into the glass bowl on top of the prawns. Sprinkle with a little paprika and serve.

BREADED MOZZARELLA CUBES

(ITALIC RESTAURANT STYLE)

Serves 1–2

3 slices of white bread, crusts removed
½ teaspoon dried Italian herbs
¼ teaspoon garlic powder
½ teaspoon onion powder
Pinch of cayenne pepper
¼ teaspoon black pepper
125 g/4 oz mozzarella cheese
4 tablespoons plain flour
1 egg
50 ml/2 fl oz milk

In a blender, combine the white bread (crusts removed), dried Italian herbs, garlic powder, onion powder, cayenne pepper and black pepper. Blitz well. Pour the seasoned breadcrumbs into a large bowl and set aside.

Cut the mozzarella cheese into 7–8 cubes.

Spread the plain flour over a plate. In a separate bowl, combine the egg and milk and mix thoroughly.

Keeping one hand dry, dip the cheese cubes first into the plain flour, then into the egg and milk mixture, and finally into the seasoned breadcrumbs.

Deep fry the breaded cheese cubes in hot oil on a medium-high heat for around 2–3 minutes or until the breadcrumbs begin to turn golden. Once cooked, remove the mozzarella cubes from the pan and drain off any excess oil.

Arrange the breaded mozzarella cubes on a plate and serve with a selection of dips.

VEGETABLE PAKORA

(INDIAN RESTAURANT STYLE)

Serves 1–2

Almost any vegetables will work well in this dish and the spice level can be increased if a hotter pakora is desired. Fresh chopped coriander may also be used instead of dried fenugreek leaves if preferred.

1 potato
1 onion
1 handful of finely chopped cabbage or spinach leaves
2 teaspoons coriander seeds
2 teaspoons cumin seeds
½ teaspoon chilli powder
½ teaspoon garam masala
1 teaspoon dried fenugreek leaves
¼ teaspoon salt
1 tablespoon tomato ketchup
1 tablespoon natural yogurt
2–3 tablespoons water
8–10 tablespoons gram flour
Oil for deep frying
Thinly sliced onions and lemon for garnish

Peel and finely chop the potato and onion. Add the chopped cabbage or spinach leaves.

Add the coriander seeds, cumin seeds, chilli powder, garam masala, dried fenugreek leaves and salt. Set aside for 20 minutes.

Add the tomato ketchup and natural yogurt. Mix well. Add the water and gram flour a little at a time. Mix thoroughly, adding a little more water or gram flour if necessary until the desired consistency is reached. The mixture should form a thick paste which will drop off the back of a tablespoon.

Heat the oil on a medium-high heat. Drop tablespoons of the pakora batter into the hot oil. Cook the pakora in batches, making sure not to overcrowd the pan. Fry for 5–6 minutes or until the pakora has turned golden and begins to darken, turning the pakora pieces occasionally.

Remove the pakora pieces from the pan and drain off any excess oil. Serve garnished with thinly sliced onions and lemon slices, with kebab and pakora sauces (pages 128–30).

CHICKEN PAKORA
(INDIAN RESTAURANT STYLE)

Serves 2–3

Mildly spiced chicken pieces coated in a crispy gram flour batter.

2 large skinless, boneless chicken breast fillets (around
   113 g/4 oz weight per fillet)
1 teaspoon vegetable oil
1 teaspoon garlic and ginger paste
2 teaspoons tomato purée
2 teaspoons lemon juice
Pinch of salt
125 g/4 oz gram flour
1 tablespoon dried fenugreek leaves
1 large handful of chopped fresh coriander leaves
2 teaspoons cumin powder
½ teaspoon chilli powder
1 teaspoon salt
120 ml/4 fl oz water
Oil for deep frying
Thinly sliced onion and lemon slices to garnish

Trim any excess fat from the chicken breasts and cut into bite sized pieces. Add the vegetable oil, garlic and ginger paste, tomato purée, lemon juice and salt. Mix well and set aside.

In a large bowl, combine the gram flour, dried fenugreek leaves, fresh coriander, cumin powder, chilli powder and salt. Mix well. Add the water a little at a time until a smooth, thick batter is created. The consistency should be similar to that of double cream.

Add the chicken pieces and allow to rest in the batter for 20 minutes.

Heat the oil on a medium-high heat. Drop the coated chicken pieces into the hot oil. Cook the pakora in batches, making sure not to overcrowd the pan. Fry for 5–6 minutes or until the batter turns golden and the chicken is cooked through, turning the pakora pieces occasionally.

Remove the chicken pakora pieces from the pan and drain off any excess oil. Arrange the pakora on a plate or serving tray and garnish with sliced onion and lemon slices. Serve with Pakora Sauce (page 130).

BREADED CHICKEN STRIPS

(KEBAB SHOP STYLE)

Serves 1

These tender chicken breast strips are coated in seasoned breadcrumbs and make an ideal side dish served with potato wedges and pizza.

3 slices of white bread, crusts removed
¼ teaspoon garlic powder
¼ teaspoon onion powder
½ teaspoon dried Italian herbs
Pinch of black pepper
4 tablespoons plain flour
1 egg
120 ml/4 fl oz milk
1 large skinless, boneless chicken breast fillet (around
    113 g/4 oz weight)
Oil for deep frying

In a blender, combine the white bread (crusts removed), garlic powder, onion powder, dried Italian herbs and black pepper. Blitz well. Pour the seasoned breadcrumbs into a large bowl and set aside.

Spread the plain flour over a plate. In a separate bowl, combine the egg and milk and mix thoroughly.

Trim any excess fat from the chicken breast and cut into 5–6 long strips.

Keeping one hand dry, dip the chicken strips first into the plain flour, then into the egg and milk mixture, and finally into the seasoned breadcrumbs.

Deep fry the chicken pieces in hot oil on a medium-high heat for around 5–6 minutes or until the breadcrumbs begin to turn golden and the chicken is cooked through. Lower the heat a little during cooking if the breadcrumbs begin to colour too quickly. Once cooked, remove the chicken strips from the pan and drain off any excess oil.

Alternatively, place the breaded chicken strips on a lightly oiled baking tray and cook at 220°C/425°F/Gas Mark 7 for 15–20 minutes or until the chicken is cooked through.

Arrange the chicken strips on a plate and serve with a selection of dips.

SOUTHERN FRIED CHICKEN

(AMERICAN FAST-FOOD STYLE)

Serves 1–2

This classic chicken dish spawned a global fast-food chain. Cook the chicken pieces in batches if necessary to avoid overcrowding the pan.

120 g/4 oz plain flour
2 teaspoons garlic powder
½ teaspoon onion powder
½ teaspoon paprika
1 teaspoon salt
½ teaspoon black pepper
1 egg
100 ml/3½ fl oz milk
50 ml/2 fl oz water
5–6 chicken pieces (thighs and drumsticks)
Oil for deep frying

In a large bowl or food-safe bag, combine the plain flour, garlic powder, onion powder, paprika, salt and black pepper. Mix well.

In a separate bowl, combine the egg, milk and water. Whisk thoroughly until well combined.

Keeping one hand dry, dip the chicken pieces first into the seasoned flour, then into the egg, milk and water mixture, and finally into the seasoned flour again. Repeat this process until all of the chicken pieces have been coated twice in the seasoned flour.

At this stage, the coated chicken pieces may be refrigerated for 1–2 hours. This is optional, but will help ensure that the coating sticks to the chicken pieces when deep fried.

Deep fry the chicken pieces in hot oil on a medium-high heat for around 7–8 minutes or until the coating begins to seal around the chicken pieces.

Turn the chicken pieces, lower the heat to medium and cook for a further 7–8 minutes or until the coating is golden and the chicken is cooked though.

Once cooked, remove the chicken pieces from the pan and drain off any excess oil. Serve with coleslaw and French fries.

HONEY BARBECUE WINGS

(KEBAB SHOP STYLE)

Serves 1–2

6 tablespoons tomato ketchup
1 teaspoon white vinegar
2 tablespoons soy sauce
2 tablespoons Worcester sauce
1 teaspoon Tabasco sauce
1 teaspoon Dijon mustard
4 tablespoons water
2 tablespoons honey
1 teaspoon garlic powder
½ tablespoon smoked paprika
¼ teaspoon black pepper
2 tablespoons vegetable oil
6 chicken wings, split into 12 wing pieces and tips discarded
Lemon slices for garnish

In a bowl, combine the tomato ketchup, white vinegar, soy sauce, Worcester sauce, Tabasco sauce, Dijon mustard, water, honey, garlic powder, smoked paprika and black pepper. Mix thoroughly.

Reserve 2 tablespoons of the marinade in a separate bowl for basting if desired.

Add the vegetable oil and the chicken wing pieces. Rub the marinade thoroughly into each chicken wing piece. Cover the bowl and refrigerate for at least 4 hours, or overnight if possible.

Preheat the oven to 200°C/400°F/Gas Mark 6.

Arrange the chicken wings on a baking tray. Bake in the middle of the oven for 15 minutes.

Turn the chicken pieces and cook for a further 15 minutes.

If some marinade was reserved for basting, brush it onto the wings now. Turn the chicken pieces again, move to the top of the oven and cook for 5–6 minutes.

Baste once more, turn the chicken pieces for a final time and return to the top of the oven for a further 5–6 minutes.

Remove the chicken wings from the oven and arrange on a plate or serving dish. Serve with a few slices of lemon.

CHICKEN NUGGETS

(AMERICAN FAST-FOOD STYLE)

Serves 1

Chicken nuggets are a classic American fast-food snack which has spawned countless variations. This recipe is based on modern day chicken nuggets which are made from cuts of whole breast meat.

120 g/4 oz plain flour
1 teaspoon onion powder
½ teaspoon garlic powder
1 teaspoon salt
½ teaspoon black pepper
1 egg
120 ml/4 fl oz milk
1 large skinless, boneless chicken breast fillet (around
    113 g/4 oz weight)
Oil for deep frying

In a bowl, combine the plain flour, onion powder, garlic powder, salt and black pepper. In a separate bowl, combine the egg and milk.

Using a meat mallet, pound the chicken breast fillet until thin. Use scissors to cut the chicken into small bite sized pieces. Keeping one hand dry, dip the chicken pieces first into the seasoned flour, then into the egg and milk mixture, and finally into the seasoned flour once again.

Leave to rest for a few minutes and repeat the process again if desired for a thicker coating.

Fry the chicken nuggets in hot oil on a medium heat for around 5–6 minutes or until golden brown and cooked through. Remove the chicken from the pan and drain off any excess oil.

Arrange the nuggets on a plate or in a serving tub and serve with a selection of dips.

SPICY CHICKEN WINGS

(Kebab Shop Style)

Serves 1–2

1 teaspoon cayenne pepper
¼ teaspoon chilli powder
1 tablespoon smoked paprika
2 teaspoons garlic powder
2 teaspoons onion powder
1 teaspoon dried oregano
1 teaspoon dried thyme
¾ teaspoon salt
¼ teaspoon black pepper
4 tablespoons vegetable oil
1 tablespoon lemon juice
6 chicken wings, split into 12 wing pieces and tips discarded
Lemon slices for garnish

In a large bowl, combine the cayenne pepper, chilli powder, smoked paprika, garlic powder, onion powder, dried oregano, dried thyme, salt and black pepper.

Add the vegetable oil, lemon juice and chicken wing pieces. Rub the marinade thoroughly into each chicken wing piece. Cover the bowl and refrigerate for at least 4 hours, or overnight if possible.

Preheat the oven to 200°C/400°F/Gas Mark 6.

Arrange the chicken wings on a baking tray. Bake in the middle of the oven for 15 minutes.

Turn the chicken pieces and cook for a further 15 minutes.

Turn the chicken pieces again, move to the top of the oven and cook for 5–6 minutes.

Turn the chicken pieces for a final time and return to the top of the oven for a further 5–6 minutes.

Remove the chicken wings from the oven and arrange on a plate or serving dish. Serve with lemon slices.

SALT AND PEPPER CHILLI CHICKEN WINGS

(CHINESE TAKEAWAY STYLE)

Serves 1–2

1 tablespoon Szechuan peppercorns
½ teaspoon black pepper
½ teaspoon sea salt
6 chicken wings, split into 12 wing pieces and tips discarded
1 teaspoon vegetable oil
Pinch of salt
Pinch of black pepper
2 tablespoons vegetable oil
½ onion, chopped
½ green pepper, chopped
2 cloves of garlic, finely chopped
2 finger chilli peppers, sliced (see page 39)
2 tablespoons tomato ketchup (recommended brand: Heinz)
2 tablespoons sweet chilli sauce
4 tablespoons water
1 spring onion, finely sliced
Lemon slices for garnish

Heat a dry, flat frying pan over a medium heat and add the Szechuan peppercorns. Toast the peppercorns for 2–3 minutes, stirring occasionally. Remove from the heat, crush with a pestle and mortar and mix with the black pepper and sea salt. Set aside.

Preheat the oven to 200°C/400°F/Gas Mark 6.

Arrange the chicken wings on a baking tray. Rub the vegetable oil, salt and black pepper into the wings. Bake in the middle of the oven for 15 minutes.

Turn the chicken pieces and cook for a further 15 minutes.

Remove the cooked wings from the oven and set aside for 2–3 minutes.

Heat the 2 tablespoons of oil in a frying pan over a medium heat. Add the chicken wings, onion and green pepper. Stir-fry for 2–3 minutes.

Add the sliced garlic and chilli peppers. Stir-fry for a further 1 minute.

Add the tomato ketchup, sweet chilli sauce and water, tossing the pan to ensure the chicken wings are fully coated. Season the wings to taste with the prepared Szechuan pepper and salt mixture. Stir-fry for another 1–2 minutes or until the sauce begins to thicken around the wings.

Pour the chicken wings, vegetables and sauce onto a plate or serving tray. Sprinkle the spring onion slices over the wings and serve with lemon slices.

HONEY SOY CHICKEN WINGS

(CHINESE TAKEAWAY STYLE)

Serves 1–2

1 teaspoon garlic and ginger paste
4 tablespoons soy sauce
2 tablespoons lemon juice
1 tablespoon honey
½ teaspoon Chinese five-spice powder
2 tablespoons vegetable oil
6 chicken wings, split into 12 wing pieces and tips discarded
Lemon slices for garnish

In a large bowl, combine the garlic and ginger paste, soy sauce, lemon juice, honey and Chinese five-spice.

Add the vegetable oil and the chicken wing pieces. Rub the marinade thoroughly into each chicken wing piece. Cover the bowl and refrigerate for at least 4 hours, or overnight if possible.

Preheat the oven to 200°C/400°F/Gas Mark 6.

Arrange the chicken wings on a baking tray. Bake in the middle of the oven for 15 minutes.

Turn the chicken pieces and cook for a further 15 minutes.

Turn the chicken pieces again, move to the top of the oven and cook for 5–6 minutes.

Turn the chicken pieces for a final time and return to the top of the oven for a further 5–6 minutes.

Remove the chicken wings from the oven and arrange on a plate or serving dish. Serve with lemon slices.

BUFFALO WINGS

(AMERICAN FAST-FOOD STYLE)

Serves 1–2

These classic wings are named after their city of origin, Buffalo, New York. The fried wings are tossed in a butter based hot sauce and served with celery sticks and blue cheese dip. Many takeaway restaurants in America now also offer 'boneless wings'. These are made not from wings but from boneless chicken breast fillets, breaded and fried, and coated in the classic buffalo hot sauce.

120 g/4 oz plain flour
½ teaspoon paprika
¼ teaspoon cayenne pepper
¼ teaspoon salt
4 tablespoons butter
4 tablespoons hot sauce (recommended brand: Franks Red Hot Cayenne Pepper Sauce)
¼ teaspoon garlic powder
6 chicken wings, split into 12 wing pieces and tips discarded
Oil for deep frying

In a large bowl, combine the plain flour, paprika, cayenne pepper and salt. Set aside.

In a small pot, combine the butter, hot pepper sauce and garlic powder over a low heat until the butter is melted. Mix well.

Toss the chicken wing pieces in the bowl of seasoned flour. Deep fry the chicken pieces in hot oil on a medium heat for around 8–10 minutes or until the chicken is cooked through.

Once cooked, remove the chicken pieces from the pan and drain off any excess oil. Dip each wing piece into the prepared sauce until well coated.

Arrange the Buffalo wings on a plate or serving dish. Serve with celery sticks and blue cheese dressing.

SPARE RIBS

(Chinese Takeaway Style)

Serves 1–2

These classic Chinese ribs are flavoured with five-spice powder and can be served dry or with Chinese brown gravy (page 76).

2 teaspoons garlic and ginger paste
8 tablespoons tomato ketchup
3 tablespoons honey
½ tablespoon Chinese five-spice powder
1 kg/2.2 lb pork ribs

In a bowl, combine the garlic and ginger paste, tomato ketchup, honey and Chinese five-spice. Mix well.

Add the pork ribs to the marinade and mix well until all of the ribs are coated. Marinade for at least 4 hours or overnight if possible.

Preheat the oven to 200°C/400°F/Gas Mark 6. Arrange the pork ribs on a rack over a roasting tray filled with a little water.

Place the ribs onto the middle oven shelf and bake for 8 minutes.

Turn the ribs and cook for a further 8 minutes.

Turn the ribs once more, move to the top of the oven and cook for 8 minutes.

Turn the ribs for a final time and return to the top of the oven for a further 8 minutes or until the ribs are charred and cooked through.

Remove the ribs from the oven and arrange on a plate or serving dish. Serve as a starter or side dish with any Chinese meal.

SWEET AND SOUR RIBS

(CHINESE TAKEAWAY STYLE)

Serves 1–2

4 tablespoons tomato ketchup
100 ml/3½ fl oz pineapple juice
1 ½ tablespoons white vinegar
2 tablespoons brown sugar
1 tablespoon honey
2 teaspoons soy sauce (recommended brand: Kikkoman)
2 teaspoons cornflour
1 kg/2.2 lb pork ribs

In a small pan, combine the tomato ketchup, pineapple juice, white vinegar, brown sugar, honey, soy sauce and cornflour. Mix well and bring to a boil. Turn the heat to low and simmer for 2 minutes or until the marinade just starts to thicken.

Allow the mixture to cool slightly. Reserve 2 tablespoons of the marinade in a separate bowl for basting.

Add the pork ribs and mix well until all of the ribs are coated.

Preheat the oven to 200°C/400°F/Gas Mark 6. Arrange the pork ribs on a rack over a roasting tray filled with a little water.

Bake in the middle of the oven for 8 minutes.

Turn the ribs and cook for a further 8 minutes.

Turn the ribs once more, move to the top of the oven and cook for 8 minutes.

Brush the ribs with the reserved marinade. Turn the ribs for a final time and return to the top of the oven for a further 8 minutes or until the ribs are charred and cooked through.

Remove the ribs from the oven and arrange on a plate or serving dish. Serve the ribs as a starter or side dish with any Chinese meal.

VEGETABLE PANCAKE ROLLS

(Chinese Takeaway Style)

Serves 3 (makes around 5–6 pancake rolls)

Any leftover cooked meats or vegetables may be added to the filling mixture for these pancake or 'spring' rolls.

120 g/4 oz plain flour
160 ml/5½ fl oz cold water
¼ teaspoon salt
1 tablespoon vegetable oil
1 carrot, grated
1 large handful of bean sprouts
2–3 button mushrooms, sliced
¼ red pepper, finely sliced
Small handful of rice noodles, softened in water and drained
1 small handful of shredded white cabbage leaves
1 teaspoon soy sauce (recommended brand: Kikkoman)
Pinch of black pepper
1 tablespoon cornflour, mixed with 2 tablespoons water
Oil for deep frying

In a large bowl, combine the plain flour, cold water and salt. Mix thoroughly to create a thin batter. Add a little more water if required until the batter reaches the desired consistency. It should be very slightly thick.

Heat a lightly oiled frying pan over a medium-low heat. Pour a large tablespoon of batter into the pan and immediately tilt to create a large, thin, circular pancake. Cook the pancake on one side only for around 1 minute or until the edges begin to curl. Remove from the pan and set aside.

Repeat the process with the remaining batter until all of the spring roll wrappers are ready.

At this stage, the spring roll wrappers may be used immediately, or frozen for up to 1 month.

To create a filling for the spring rolls, heat 1 tablespoon of vegetable oil over a medium-high heat. Add the grated carrot, bean sprouts, sliced mushrooms, red pepper, rice noodles and shredded white cabbage leaves. Stir-fry for 3–4 minutes.

Add the soy sauce and black pepper and stir-fry for a further 1 minute.

Remove the cooked ingredients from the pan and set aside to cool.

To assemble and cook the finished pancake rolls, take a spoonful of the filling mixture and place it close to the bottom of the pancake wrapper. Fold the bottom of the wrapper over the filling and then fold in both the left and right edges and continue rolling towards the top of the wrapper.

Brush the top of the pancake roll wrapper with a little of the cornflour and water mixture. Seal the pancake roll tightly.

Deep fry the pancake rolls in hot oil over a medium-high heat for 3–4 minutes or until golden. Drain off any excess oil and arrange the cooked pancake rolls on a wire rack over a baking tray for 2–3 minutes. This will ensure that the pastry batter does not become soggy.

Arrange the pancake rolls on a plate and serve as a side dish with any Chinese meal.

PRAWN TOAST

(CHINESE TAKEAWAY STYLE)

Serves 3

175 g/6 oz cooked, peeled prawns
2 spring onions
1 tablespoon garlic and ginger paste
2 tablespoons cornflour
2 teaspoons soy sauce (recommended brand: Kikkoman)
6 slices of white bread, crusts removed
40 g/1½ oz sesame seeds
Oil for deep frying

Add the cooked prawns, spring onions, garlic and ginger paste, cornflour and soy sauce into a blender. Blitz for 30–40 seconds until a paste is formed.

Spread the paste onto the bread slices. Cut each slice into triangles. Pour the sesame seeds onto a plate, then press the bread slices down so that the seeds stick to the paste.

Reserve the bread triangles in the fridge for around 1 hour. This will help ensure that the prawn and sesame seed mixture sticks to the bread.

Heat the oil for deep frying to a medium heat. Drop the bread slices into the oil and fry for 2–3 minutes, turning half way through cooking.

Remove the bread slices from the pan and drain off any excess oil. Serve with Chinese Dipping Sauce (page 130).

CHICKEN NOODLE SOUP

(CHINESE TAKEAWAY STYLE)

Serves 2–3

1 litre/1¾ pints light chicken stock (or 1 litre of water mixed
    with 1 chicken stock cube)
1 clove of garlic, finely chopped
1 x 2.5 cm/1 inch piece of ginger, finely chopped
1 skinless, boneless chicken breast fillet
1–2 chestnut mushrooms, thinly sliced
½ finger chilli pepper (optional), sliced (see page 39)
3 tablespoons sweetcorn (tinned or frozen)
1–2 spring onions, sliced
1 teaspoon soy sauce (recommended brand: Kikkoman)
1 nest of egg noodles
Fresh coriander to garnish

In a large pan, bring the chicken stock to boiling point. Reduce the heat
to low. Add the chopped garlic and ginger.

Trim any excess fat from the chicken breast and add it to the pan. Cover
the pan with a lid and simmer on a low heat for 7–8 minutes or until
the chicken breast is cooked through.

Remove the cooked chicken from the pan and use a knife and fork to
shred into small pieces. Return the shredded chicken to the pan.

Add the mushrooms, chilli pepper, sweetcorn and half of the spring
onions to the pan, reserving the remaining spring onions for garnish.

Add the soy sauce. Simmer for a further 4–5 minutes.

Add the nest of egg noodles to the pan and simmer for a further 3–4
minutes, stirring occasionally to separate the noodles. Ladle the soup
into serving bowls, ensuring the chicken, vegetables and noodles are
evenly distributed. Garnish with the remaining spring onions and a little
fresh coriander. Serve with a little extra soy sauce on the side.

ONION RINGS

(KEBAB SHOP STYLE)

Serves 1–2

These crispy battered onion rings are best prepared with large Spanish onion slices. In takeaway restaurants, the large outer onion rings are often reserved for use in this dish, while the smaller inner slices are chopped and sliced for various other dishes.

120 g/4 oz plain flour
1 teaspoon baking powder
½ teaspoon salt
¼ teaspoon black pepper
1 egg
200 ml/7 fl oz milk
2 slices of white bread, crusts removed
1 large onion

In a large bowl, combine the plain flour, baking powder, salt and black pepper. Mix well. In a separate bowl, combine the egg and milk. Whisk thoroughly.

Add the bread slices to a blender. Blitz well. Pour the breadcrumbs into a large bowl and set aside.

Slice the onion into large rings. Coat each onion ring in the flour mixture and set aside.

Add the egg and milk mixture to the flour. Mix well; adding more milk if necessary until a medium thick batter is created.

Keeping one hand dry, dip the floured onion rings first into the batter mixture and then into the breadcrumbs. Repeat this process until all of the onion rings have been coated in breadcrumbs.

Deep fry the onion rings in hot oil on a medium heat for around 2–3 minutes or until golden.

Once cooked, remove the onion rings from the pan and drain off any excess oil. Serve with White Kebab Sauce (page 129).

GARLIC MUSHROOMS

(KEBAB SHOP STYLE)

Serves 1–2

120 g/4 oz plain flour
½ teaspoon salt
1 egg
200 ml/7 fl oz milk
2 slices of white bread, crusts removed
¼ teaspoon garlic powder
¼ teaspoon onion powder
¼ teaspoon dried Italian herbs
Pinch of cayenne pepper
Pinch of black pepper
10–12 small button mushrooms

In a large bowl, combine the plain flour and salt. Mix well.

In a separate bowl, combine the egg and milk. Whisk thoroughly.

In a blender, combine the white bread, garlic powder, onion powder, Italian herbs, cayenne pepper and black pepper. Blitz well. Pour the breadcrumbs into a large bowl and set aside.

Clean the mushrooms with a brush or kitchen paper. Coat each mushroom in the flour mixture and set aside.

Add the egg and milk mixture to the flour. Mix well; adding more milk if necessary until a medium thick batter is created.

Keeping one hand dry, dip the floured mushrooms first into the batter mixture and then into the breadcrumbs. Repeat this process until all of the mushrooms have been coated in breadcrumbs.

Deep fry the mushrooms in hot oil on a medium heat for around 2–3 minutes or until golden.

Once cooked, remove the mushrooms from the pan and drain off any excess oil. Serve with White Kebab Sauce (page 129).

FILLED POTATO SKINS WITH BACON

(KEBAB SHOP STYLE)

Serves 1–2

It's worth taking the time to bake the potatoes in the oven and grill the bacon. If time is short, however, both may be cooked in the microwave.

2 large baking potatoes
1 teaspoon vegetable oil
Pinch of sea salt
4 slices of bacon
1 tablespoon butter
1 tablespoon cream
2 handfuls of grated cheese
Pinch of sea salt
Pinch of black pepper
Pinch of paprika powder
2 spring onions, sliced

Preheat the oven to 200°C/400°F/Gas Mark 6. Wash and dry the baking potatoes. Pierce each potato several times and rub with vegetable oil and sea salt. Place directly onto the middle rack of the oven for 1 hour or until the skin is crisp and the potatoes are soft on the inside.

Grill the bacon slices under a medium-hot grill for 4–6 minutes or until crispy. Turn the bacon half way through cooking. Set aside.

Remove the potatoes from the oven and set aside to cool for 5 minutes. Slice each potato and use a spoon to scoop the flesh into a bowl. Add the butter, cream, grated cheese, salt and pepper and mix well.

Spoon the potato mixture back into the potato skins. Grate a little extra cheese over the top. Return to the oven and bake for a further 10–15 minutes.

Place the filled potato skins onto a plate or serving dish. Sprinkle with a pinch of paprika. Break the bacon into pieces and crumble over the top of the potatoes. Garnish with the sliced spring onions and serve.

POTATO WEDGES

(KEBAB SHOP STYLE)

Serves 1–2

The ideal accompaniment to pizza and breaded chicken strips; Maris Peer and Maris Piper potatoes provide excellent results in this recipe.

2 potatoes
1 tablespoon olive oil
½ tablespoon plain flour
¼ teaspoon garlic powder
¼ teaspoon onion powder
Pinch of salt
Pinch of black pepper

Preheat the oven to 220°C/425°F/Gas Mark 7.

Wash and dry the potatoes, leaving the skin on. Cut each potato in half lengthways, then into quarters. Slice each quarter once more to create 8 wedges per potato.

Place the potato wedges in a bowl and add the olive oil, flour, garlic powder, onion powder, salt and pepper. Mix well.

Arrange the potato wedges on a lightly greased baking tray and cook in the middle of the oven for 25–30 minutes or until cooked through, turning occasionally.

Serve with a selection of dips.

OVEN BAKED GARLIC BREAD

(Kebab Shop Style)

Serves 1–2

1 tablespoon butter
2 tablespoons olive oil
½ teaspoon garlic powder
¼ teaspoon onion powder
½ teaspoon dried Italian herbs or dried parsley
Pinch of salt
Pinch of black pepper
3–4 large slices of ciabatta bread

Heat the oven to 220°C/425°F/Gas Mark 7.

In a bowl, combine the butter, olive oil, garlic powder, onion powder, Italian herbs or parsley, salt and black pepper. Mix thoroughly until well combined.

Arrange the bread slices on a baking tray. Spread each slice generously with the garlic butter mixture.

Place the tray in the oven for 7–8 minutes or until the bread is crispy and golden.

Remove the tray from the oven, leave to rest for 2–3 minutes and serve.

Variation

GARLIC BREAD WITH CHEESE

After spreading the bread slices with garlic butter, add a small handful of grated mozzarella cheese. Bake as normal until the cheese is golden.

CORN ON THE COB

(MEXICAN STYLE)

Serves 1–2

Before smothering in butter, finish these corn cobs on a griddle pan or outdoor barbecue if desired to add a delicious smoky flavour.

1 tablespoon sugar
2 fresh corn cobs, husks removed
2 tablespoons butter
Pinch of salt
Pinch of black pepper

Fill a large pan with water and bring to the boil. Add the sugar and mix well.

Add the corn cobs and reduce the heat to low. Simmer for 5–6 minutes or until soft.

Remove the corn cobs from the water and drain on kitchen paper.

Spread the butter onto a serving plate. Turn the corn cobs in the butter until coated.

Add salt and pepper to taste and serve.

QUESADILLA

(MEXICAN STYLE)

Serves 1–2

Any good Cheddar or mozzarella cheese will work very well in this recipe. Add serrano ham or sliced chilli peppers to the quesadilla if desired.

2 large flour tortillas
1 large handful of grated cheese

Heat a lightly oiled frying pan over a medium heat. Put one flour tortilla in the pan and cook for 30 seconds.

Turn the flour tortilla over and add the grated cheese evenly over the surface. Add the remaining flour tortilla and press down gently. Continue cooking for a further 1–2 minutes.

Flip the quesadilla over and cook for a further 1 minute.

Remove the quesadilla from the pan and use a pizza cutter to slice into 4 large triangles. Serve with Pico De Gallo (page 138).

PITTA SALAD

(KEBAB SHOP STYLE)

Serves 2–3

The jarred chilli peppers used to finish this kebab shop salad can be found in antipasti sections in any good supermarket.

2 red onions, finely sliced
1 carrot, grated
¼ cucumber, thinly sliced
4–5 red cabbage leaves, finely sliced
1 large handful of shredded lettuce
1 tomato, sliced
1 tablespoon lemon juice
3–4 tablespoons or to taste Red Kebab Sauce (page 128)
1–2 jalapeno chilli peppers (jarred)
3 pitta breads

Place the sliced onions in a bowl of cold water for around 30 minutes. Drain well through a sieve and pat the onion dry with kitchen paper.

In a large bowl, combine the sliced onion, grated carrot, sliced cucumber, sliced cabbage leaves, shredded lettuce and sliced tomato.

Add the lemon juice and mix well. Dress with the Red Kebab Sauce and garnish with the jalapeno peppers.

Grill the pitta breads under a hot grill for around 30 seconds on each side or until soft and heated through.

Serve the pitta salad with kebabs, kebab sauces and spiced onions.

GREEK SALAD

(KEBAB SHOP STYLE)

Serves 2

½ small red onion, finely chopped
½ cucumber, peeled and deseeded
3 plum tomatoes, seeded and chopped
10–12 black olives, sliced
1 small handful of chopped lettuce
1 tablespoon lemon juice
3 tablespoons extra virgin olive oil
½ teaspoon red wine vinegar
1 clove of garlic, finely chopped
¼ teaspoon dried oregano
¼ teaspoon salt
¼ teaspoon black pepper
125 g/4 oz feta cheese, diced

Place the chopped onion in a bowl of cold water for around 30 minutes. Drain well through a sieve and pat the onion dry with kitchen paper.

In a large bowl, combine the red onion, cucumber, plum tomatoes, black olives and lettuce.

In a small bowl, combine the lemon juice, extra virgin olive oil, red wine vinegar, chopped garlic, dried oregano, salt and black pepper. Mix well.

Pour as much dressing as desired over the prepared salad ingredients. Mix well.

Top the salad with the feta cheese cubes and serve with toasted pitta bread.

TURMERIC RICE

(INDIAN RESTAURANT STYLE)

Serves 1–2

100 g/3½ oz basmati rice (uncooked weight)
¼ teaspoon turmeric
Pinch of salt

Wash the rice thoroughly in cold water until the water runs clear.

Fill a large pan with water and bring to the boil. Add the turmeric and salt.

Add the rice and allow the pan to return to boiling. Stir the rice once only to prevent it from sticking. Simmer for 7–8 minutes or until the rice is cooked.

When the rice is cooked, drain almost all of the water away. Put a lid on the pan and allow the rice to rest for 2–3 minutes. After resting, the rice should be dry.

Use a fork to stir the rice and pour into a bowl or serving tub. Serve with any Indian curry.

PILAU RICE

(INDIAN RESTAURANT STYLE)

Serves 1–2

This fragrant rice is the perfect partner to any Indian curry dish. If desired, add a selection of vegetables, such as mushrooms and green peas, to create a vegetarian main course.

100 g/3½ oz basmati rice (uncooked weight)
1–2 tablespoons vegetable oil
1 small onion, finely chopped
1 tomato, thinly sliced
1 clove of garlic, finely chopped
1 cinnamon stick
2 bay leaves
4 cloves
1 teaspoon coriander powder
Pinch of ginger powder
Pinch of salt
¼ teaspoon black pepper

Wash the rice thoroughly in cold water until the water runs clear. Fill a large pan with water and bring to the boil. Add the rice and allow the pan to return to boiling. Stir the rice once only to prevent it from sticking. Simmer for 7–8 minutes or until the rice is cooked.

Drain the rice and rinse with cold water. Drain again and place the rice in a covered bowl or container. Place in the fridge for at least 4 hours or overnight if possible.

Add the vegetable oil to the pan over a medium-high heat. Add the onion and stir-fry for 5–6 minutes until just beginning to darken. Add the sliced tomato, finely chopped garlic, cinnamon stick, bay leaves, cloves, coriander powder, ginger powder, salt and black pepper. Stir-fry for 2 minutes.

Add the cooked, cooled rice to the pan and immediately stir-fry to ensure all the grains of rice are coated in oil. Continue to stir-fry for a further 2–3 minutes.

Serve with any Indian curry.

FRIED RICE

(CHINESE TAKEAWAY STYLE)

Serves 1–2

This recipe will provide perfect fried rice every time, ideal to serve with any Chinese main meal. Add a selection of chopped vegetables, such as mushrooms, onions, carrots, etc, to create a vegetable fried rice main course.

100 g/3½ oz basmati rice (uncooked weight)
1–2 tablespoons vegetable oil
2 tablespoons soy sauce
1 handful of chopped spring onions (optional)
Pinch of black pepper

Wash the rice thoroughly in cold water until the water runs clear. Fill a large pan with water and bring to the boil. Add the rice and allow the pan to return to boiling. Stir the rice once only to prevent it from sticking. Simmer for 7–8 minutes or until the rice is cooked.

Immediately drain the rice and rinse with cold water. Drain again and place the rice in a covered bowl or container. Place in the fridge for at least 4 hours or overnight if possible.

Add the vegetable oil to the pan over a medium-high heat. Add the cooked rice to the pan and immediately stir-fry to ensure all the grains of rice are coated in oil. Stir-fry for 2–3 minutes.

Add the soy sauce and continue to stir fry for a further 1–2 minutes or until the rice is thoroughly reheated and fried. Add the chopped spring onions if desired. Add the black pepper and mix thoroughly through the rice.

VARIATION

EGG FRIED RICE

Before frying the rice, crack an egg into the hot pan and immediately stir-fry, breaking the egg up into pieces with a spatula. Remove the egg from the pan and set aside, returning to the pan just before the rice is heated through.

RED KEBAB SAUCE

(KEBAB SHOP STYLE)

Serves 1

This spicy sauce is an essential part of the kebab shop experience.

6 tablespoons tomato ketchup
4 tablespoons water
1 teaspoon mint sauce
Chilli powder to taste
Pinch of salt

In a bowl or serving tub, combine the tomato ketchup, water, mint sauce, chilli powder and salt.

Add chilli powder sparingly at first until the desired heat is obtained. Add a little more water until the sauce reaches the desired consistency.

Serve the sauce with Pitta Salad (page 123), kebabs and pakoras.

WHITE KEBAB SAUCE

(KEBAB SHOP STYLE)

Serves 1

This garlic mayonnaise and yogurt based sauce is creamy and light, ideal to serve with lamb kebabs or chicken pakora.

3 tablespoons mayonnaise
1 tablespoon natural yogurt
1 teaspoon olive oil
¼ teaspoon garlic powder
Pinch of salt
Pinch of dried parsley or dried mixed herbs
1 tablespoon water

In a bowl or serving tub, combine the mayonnaise, natural yogurt, olive oil, garlic powder, salt and dried parsley or mixed herbs. Mix thoroughly until well combined.

Add the water and mix thoroughly again until the sauce reaches the desired consistency.

Chill for 1–2 hours before serving with kebabs and pakoras.

PAKORA SAUCE

(INDIAN RESTAURANT STYLE)

Serves 2

Around 120 ml/4 fl oz natural yogurt
2 teaspoons mint sauce
4 tablespoons tomato ketchup (recommended brand: Heinz)
Pinch of chilli powder
½ teaspoon sugar
¼ teaspoon salt
Milk to dilute

In a bowl, combine the natural yogurt, mint sauce, tomato ketchup, chilli powder, sugar and salt. Mix thoroughly.

Add a little milk if necessary until the sauce reaches the desired consistency.

Chill in the fridge for at least 30 minutes before serving with vegetable and chicken pakora.

CHINESE DIPPING SAUCE

(CHINESE TAKEAWAY STYLE)

Serves 1–2

3 tablespoons soy sauce (recommended brand: Kikkoman)
1 tablespoon hoisin or barbecue sauce
1–2 tablespoons water
¼ teaspoon toasted sesame oil
1 clove of garlic, finely chopped
¼ teaspoon grated ginger
1 spring onion, finely sliced
Pinch of white sugar

In a small bowl, combine the soy sauce, hoisin or barbecue sauce, water, toasted sesame oil, garlic, ginger, spring onion and sugar.

Mix well until thoroughly combined. Refrigerate for 1 hour before serving with Prawn Toast (page 114) or Pancake Rolls (page 112).

HONEY MUSTARD SAUCE

(AMERICAN FAST-FOOD STYLE)

Serves 1–2

60 ml/2 fl oz water
1 teaspoon cornflour
2 tablespoons honey
½ tablespoon lemon juice
2 teaspoons Dijon mustard
¼ teaspoon onion powder

In a small pan, combine the water and cornflour.

Mix well, add the honey and bring the mixture to the boil, stirring frequently.

Remove the pan from the heat. Add the lemon juice, mustard and onion powder.

Mix well once again. Pour the dip into a bowl and refrigerate until needed.

Serve with chicken nuggets or breaded chicken strips.

TARTAR SAUCE

(AMERICAN FAST-FOOD STYLE)

Serves 3–4

120 ml/4 fl oz mayonnaise
1 teaspoon lemon juice
1 teaspoon finely chopped onion
2 tablespoons finely chopped gherkin

In a bowl, combine the mayonnaise, lemon juice, chopped onion and gherkin.

Mix well and refrigerate for at least 2 hours before use. Serve with any seafood, or use to dress Fish Fillet Burgers (page 23).

RAITA

(KEBAB SHOP STYLE)

Serves 2

This creamy dip will cool the palate, making it the perfect match to any spicy Indian curry.

½ tomato, peeled, deseeded and finely chopped
¼ cucumber, skin and seeds removed
1 spring onion, finely sliced
Around 120 ml/4 fl oz natural yogurt
¼ teaspoon cumin powder
¼ teaspoon coriander powder
1 small handful of chopped fresh coriander
¼ teaspoon salt

Combine the tomato, cucumber and spring onion. Add the natural yogurt, cumin powder, coriander powder and fresh coriander.

Add the salt and mix well. Refrigerate the raita for at least 2 hours before use. Serve with any Indian curry.

TZATZIKI

(KEBAB SHOP STYLE)

Serves 2

⅓ cucumber, peeled, deseeded and grated
1 tablespoon lemon juice
1 clove of garlic, finely chopped
1 teaspoon olive oil
Around 120 ml/4 fl oz natural yogurt
Pinch of salt
Pinch of paprika to garnish

Squeeze the grated cucumber to remove some of the water. Add to a bowl with the lemon juice, chopped garlic, olive oil, natural yogurt and salt. Mix well.

Refrigerate the tzatziki for at least 1 hour. Sprinkle a little paprika over the tzatziki and serve with Pitta Salad (page 123).

SPICED ONIONS

(KEBAB SHOP STYLE)

Serves 1–2

This starter is extremely addictive and the perfect introduction to any Indian meal. Any supermarket brand of tomato ketchup will provide good results in this recipe. If desired, a little of the water the onion is soaked in can be used very effectively to thin out Red Kebab Sauce.

½ **large Spanish onion, chopped**
3 **tablespoons tomato ketchup**
¾ **teaspoon mint sauce**
1 **teaspoon mango chutney**
Pinch of chilli powder
Pinch of salt

Place the chopped onion in a bowl of cold water for around 30 minutes. Drain well through a sieve and pat the onion dry with kitchen paper.

In a bowl or serving tub, combine the onion with the tomato ketchup, mint sauce, mango chutney, chilli powder and salt.

Mix thoroughly, adding a little more ketchup if necessary to ensure the onion is fully coated with sauce.

Chill the spiced onion for 30 minutes before serving with crispy poppadoms.

COLESLAW

(Kebab Shop Style)

Serves 2

¼ small onion, finely chopped
¼ head of white cabbage (roughly 200 g/8 oz), finely sliced
2 carrots, grated
Mayonnaise
½ teaspoon sugar
¼ teaspoon salt
Pinch of black pepper

Place the chopped onion in a bowl of cold water for around 30 minutes. Drain well through a sieve and pat the onion dry with kitchen paper.

In a large bowl or container, combine the chopped onion, sliced cabbage and grated carrots.

Add mayonnaise until the mixture reaches the desired consistency.

Add the sugar, salt and black pepper. Mix well once more and refrigerate for at least 24 hours before serving. Serve with fried chicken or as a side dish with kebabs.

HUMMUS

(KEBAB SHOP STYLE)

Serves 2–3

This dip makes an excellent starter served with toasted pitta breads and salad.

1 x 400g tin of chickpeas
4 tablespoons tahini paste
2 cloves of garlic
2 tablespoons lemon juice
Pinch of cayenne pepper
1 teaspoon cumin seeds
Pinch of salt and black pepper

Drain and rinse the chickpeas.

Add the drained chickpeas to a blender and pulse for 20–30 seconds until slightly blended. Add the tahini paste, garlic cloves, lemon juice, cayenne pepper, cumin seeds, salt and black pepper.

Blitz until the hummus reaches the desired consistency. If the hummus is too thick, add some water and blend again. Serve at room temperature with breadsticks or Pitta Salad (page 123).

TAHINI PASTE

(KEBAB SHOP STYLE)

Serves 2

This paste is an essential ingredient in hummus or it can be served with kebabs.

300 g/10½ oz sesame seeds
180 ml/6 fl oz olive oil

Toast the sesame seeds in a dry frying pan, or on a baking sheet in a hot oven (180°C/350°F/Gas Mark 4) for 5–6 minutes until just golden. Stir the seeds occasionally to ensure they toast evenly.

Add the toasted seeds to a blender with the olive oil. Blend well for 2 minutes or until the paste reaches the desired consistency. Scrape the sides of the blender occasionally during blending to ensure all of the paste is mixed. Add more oil if required.

The tahini paste will keep well in the refrigerator for 1–2 months.

GUACAMOLE

(MEXICAN STYLE)

Serves 1–2

This basic guacamole also works well with added chopped fresh tomatoes, garlic and chilli peppers. Place the avocado stones into the guacamole to keep the dip's bright green colour. For a thicker, more traditional guacamole, the olive oil can be omitted.

2 ripe avocados
½ small onion, finely chopped
1–2 tablespoons olive oil
¼ teaspoon salt
1 tablespoon fresh lime juice

Halve the avocados and remove the stones from inside. Remove the flesh with a spoon.

Add the avocado and chopped onion to a large bowl along with the olive oil, salt and fresh lime juice.

Mix the ingredients gently, mashing the avocado a little each time. Serve with any Mexican dish or simply with tortilla chips.

PICO DE GALLO

(Mexican Style)

Serves 1–2

Cucumber, garlic or even hot chilli sauce can be added to this salsa if desired.

2 large tomatoes, peeled, deseeded and chopped
1 small onion, chopped
1 finger chilli pepper, sliced (see page 39)
1 large handful of chopped fresh coriander
¼ teaspoon salt
Pinch of black pepper
1–2 tablespoons fresh lime juice

In a large bowl, combine the tomatoes, onion, chilli pepper, fresh coriander, salt, black pepper and lime juice.

Mix well and set aside for 1 hour to allow the flavours to combine.

Serve with any Mexican dish, or simply with tortilla chips.

CURRY SAUCE

(Chip Shop/Chinese Takeaway Style)

Serves 2–3

This medium-hot Chinese curry sauce is available both from Chinese takeaway restaurants and chip shops around the country.

Pinch of garlic powder
¼ teaspoon sugar
Pinch of turmeric
2 tablespoons plain flour
2 teaspoons hot Madras curry powder
1 teaspoon sweet paprika
¼ teaspoon chilli powder
½ teaspoon salt
2 tablespoons vegetable oil
2–3 cloves of garlic, finely chopped
1 x 2.5 cm/1 inch piece of ginger, finely chopped
Water

In a small bowl, combine the garlic powder, sugar, turmeric, plain flour, curry powder, paprika, chilli powder and salt.

Heat the vegetable oil in a small pan over a low heat. Add the chopped garlic and ginger. Stir-fry for 2–3 minutes or until just beginning to brown.

Add the bowl of combined flour, spices and salt and leave for 30 seconds. Stir-fry for a further 30 seconds. The pan's contents will become very dry.

Add water a little at a time, stirring until well combined. Continue adding water until a thin sauce is created. Bring the mixture to the boil, reduce the heat slightly and simmer for 1–2 minutes, stirring frequently until the sauce reaches the desired consistency.

Pour the sauce into a serving bowl or tray and serve with chips and fried rice or use as a base for Chinese chicken curry.

TORTILLA WRAPS

(Mexican Style)

Makes 10–12 Tortilla Wraps

360 g/12½ oz plain white flour
¾ teaspoon salt
½ tablespoon baking powder
3 tablespoons vegetable oil
230 ml/8 fl oz warm water

In a large bowl, combine the plain flour, salt and baking powder. Mix well. Add the vegetable oil and mix once more.

Slowly add the water, stirring occasionally until dough begins to form. Empty the dough onto a floured surface and knead for 3–4 minutes until smooth. Add a little more flour while kneading if necessary to prevent the dough from sticking.

Divide the dough into 10–12 pieces. Roll each piece into a ball and cover with a slightly damp cloth. Leave to rest for 30 minutes.

Heat a dry, flat frying pan to a medium-high heat. Flatten each dough ball into a circle. Use a rolling pin to roll out each piece of dough into 20–25 cm/8–10 inch round tortillas.

Add the tortilla to the hot pan. Allow to cook for around 30–40 seconds.

Flip the tortilla and immediately press down gently 3–4 times across the tortilla using a spatula. Cook for a further 20–30 seconds.

Flip the tortilla wrap once more and press down gently again. Cook for a further 20–30 seconds.

Remove the cooked tortilla wrap from the pan and set aside on a plate. Cover the plate loosely with a sheet of foil. As each tortilla is cooked, add it to the stack and cover the plate again.

The wraps may be served immediately, or allowed to cool completely and stored for future use. They will keep well in the fridge for 1–2 days, or in the freezer for up to 1 month.

To reheat, wrap the tortillas in foil and bake in a preheated oven at 200°C/400°F/Gas Mark 6 for 10 minutes.

Serve with any Mexican dish or use cold with any good sandwich filling.

CHAPATTI

(INDIAN RESTAURANT STYLE)

Makes 8 Chapattis

Soft and light flatbreads, ideal for mopping up any curry dish.

240 g/8½ oz chapatti flour
½ teaspoon salt
160 ml/5½ fl oz water
1 tablespoon vegetable oil
1 tablespoon melted butter

In a bowl, combine the chapatti flour and salt.

Add the water a little at a time and mix well until the dough comes together.

Empty the dough onto a floured surface. Add the oil and continue kneading the dough for 2–3 minutes or until smooth. Return the dough to the bowl, cover with a damp cloth and set aside to rest for 2 hours.

Divide the dough into eight pieces. Roll each piece of dough into a ball.

On a floured surface, very carefully roll each ball out into 15–20 cm/6–8 inch circles. Try not to press down with too much force when rolling the chapattis as the dough is very fragile. Roll the dough out slowly and with only a little force.

Heat a dry, flat frying pan on a medium-high heat. Place the chapatti into the pan and leave for 30–40 seconds.

Flip the chapatti over and cook for a further 20 seconds.

Flip the chapatti once more and cook for a further 30–40 seconds, applying gentle pressure to the chapatti with a spatula. The chapatti should begin to puff up and inflate.

Turn the chapatti for the final time and cook for a further 10–20 seconds.

Remove the chapatti from the pan. If serving immediately, brush the chapatti with a little melted butter. Repeat the process until all of the chapattis are cooked.

The chapatti bread can be served immediately, or cooled and stored for future use. Reheat chapattis in a hot, dry frying pan for 30–40 seconds on each side and brush with melted butter.

Serve with chicken tikka or with any Indian curry dish.

NAN BREAD

(INDIAN RESTAURANT STYLE)

Makes 4 Nan Breads

This delicious Indian bread is the perfect accompaniment to any curry dish. The bread is traditionally cooked in a tandoor oven which provides spectacular results. With a little effort, this home cooked version is a very close second. If you have a very hot grill, the nan breads may be placed under the grill to finish cooking as opposed to being turned in the frying pan.

300 g/10½ oz strong white bread flour
1 teaspoon fast acting dried yeast
5 tablespoons natural yogurt
1 tablespoon vegetable oil
125ml milk
1 teaspoon salt
2 tablespoons black onion seeds (optional)
1–2 tablespoons melted butter to finish

In a large bowl, combine the bread flour and yeast. Mix well.

Add the natural yogurt, vegetable oil and half of the milk. Set aside for 5 minutes.

Add the salt and, if desired, the black onion seeds. Mix well and slowly add the remaining milk until a soft dough is formed.

On a lightly floured board, knead the dough for 3–4 minutes, adding more flour if necessary until the dough becomes smooth. Shape the dough into a ball.

Lightly oil the bowl and return the dough to the bowl. Cover with a wet cloth and leave to rise for around 1 hour or until doubled in size.

Knock the air out of the risen dough and divide into four equal pieces. Roll each piece of dough out into a large teardrop shape, no larger than your frying pan.

Heat a dry, heavy, cast iron frying pan over a high heat until smoking. Put the rolled out nan dough into the frying pan and cook for 30 seconds.

Move the nan bread a little to ensure it does not stick to the pan and encourage even browning. Cook for a further 1 minute.

Flip the nan bread over and continue to cook on the other side for a further 1–2 minutes or until cooked through.

Remove the nan bread from the pan and arrange on a plate. If serving immediately, brush the cooked nan with melted butter. If the nan breads are being made ahead of time, leave them dry and butter them after reheating when ready to serve.

As each nan bread is cooked, stack it on top of the previous one and cover again with foil. As the nan breads cool a little they will become soft and chewy.

VARIATIONS

GARLIC AND CORIANDER NAN

Melt 2 tablespoons of butter in a bowl. Add 2 teaspoons of garlic powder. Brush the hot, cooked nan with the garlic butter and immediately garnish with chopped fresh coriander leaves.

PESHWARI NAN

Add 2 tablespoons of pistachio nuts, 2 tablespoons of desiccated coconut and 2 tablespoons of raisins to a blender. Blitz well. Add a tablespoon of the blended mixture to each piece of flattened dough. Roll out the dough carefully once again and cook as normal.

PITTA BREAD

(Kebab Shop Style)

Makes 8 Pitta Breads

400g strong white bread flour
1 teaspoon white sugar
1 teaspoon fast acting dry yeast
1 tablespoon olive oil
300 ml/10½ fl oz water
1 teaspoon salt

In a large bowl, combine the bread flour, sugar and yeast.

Add the olive oil and mix well. Add half of the warm water and mix well again.

Add the salt. Slowly add the remaining water until the dough comes together.

On a floured board, knead the dough for 3–4 minutes until smooth. Return the dough to the bowl and cover with a damp cloth. Set aside to rest for 1 hour.

Knock the air out of the risen dough, divide into 8 pieces and knead for a further 1 minute. Shape the dough into a ball once again. Place the pitta breads onto a baking tray, cover once again and set aside for 20 minutes.

Preheat the oven to 240°C/475°F/Gas Mark 9.

Bake the pitta breads for 7–8 minutes or until puffed up and golden. Remove from the oven and wrap with a clean, damp dishcloth. This will help the pitta breads to soften a little.

Serve with any kebabs or simply toasted with hummus.

POPPADOMS

(INDIAN RESTAURANT STYLE)

Serves 1–2

Making poppadoms from scratch is a time-consuming process as the prepared dough requires to be dried for several hours before the poppadoms are ready to be cooked. A good compromise, however, is to purchase poppadoms which have been dried but not cooked.

Oil for deep frying
3–4 large poppadoms (recommended brand: TRS)

Heat the oil for deep frying on a medium-high heat. Test the oil by frying a piece of poppadom. It should react in the oil and open out immediately.

Fry the poppadoms for 2–3 seconds or until cooked. Stand the poppadoms on kitchen paper for a few minutes to remove any excess oil.

Serve with any Indian curry dish, or simply with spiced onions or mango chutney.

9

BREAKFAST AND LUNCH

Takeaway food eaten for lunch offers a convenient and quick meal, particularly handy for those of us who find ourselves rushing around in the morning before work. Many people spend a large portion of their wages simply on the food they purchase while at work which can be very frustrating.

With a little advance preparation, deli-style sandwiches and snacks can easily be created at home the night before work, saving you money and allowing you the chance to relax for your entire lunch break without the need to hunt for a decent lunchtime meal!

While it's true that a sandwich is just a sandwich, with a little inside knowledge and know how, your sandwiches and wraps will soon be elevated to deli-style status. Sandwich bars are thoughtful about how they prepare their sandwiches and know which breads and fillings combine best, as the recipes included in this chapter will show.

Many takeaway and fast-food restaurants offer a breakfast menu, with some of the most famous dishes on offer included in this chapter. Made at home, however, there's no 10:30 am cut off point to worry about, leaving you free to enjoy your favourite breakfast muffin at any time of the day!

EGG MUFFIN

(AMERICAN FAST-FOOD STYLE)

Serves 1

1 English muffin
1 teaspoon butter
1 processed cheese slice
1 egg

Slice the English muffin in half. Heat a dry, flat frying pan to a medium heat. Toast the muffins face down in the pan for around 30 seconds or until golden.

Spread the muffins with butter while they are still warm and place the processed cheese slice on the bottom half. Set aside.

Add a little oil to the pan. Using a greased egg ring, crack an egg into the pan and immediately burst the yoke with a knife. Cover the egg ring with a square of foil and cook on a low-medium heat for 2–3 minutes or until just beginning to set.

Remove the foil and the egg ring, flip the egg and continue to cook on the other side for a further 1 minute.

Remove the egg from the pan and place on the cheese topped muffin. Add the top half of the muffin and wrap in greaseproof paper or foil.

Place the wrapped muffin into an oven preheated to its lowest setting and warm through for 3–4 minutes. Serve with freshly squeezed orange juice.

VARIATIONS

BACON AND EGG MUFFIN

Add two slices of cooked Canadian bacon.

SAUSAGE AND EGG MUFFIN

Add one American breakfast sausage.

AMERICAN BREAKFAST SAUSAGE

(AMERICAN FAST-FOOD STYLE)

Serves 1

Roughly 56 g/2 oz pork mince
½ teaspoon dried sage
¼ teaspoon brown sugar
Pinch of salt
Pinch of black pepper

In a bowl, combine the pork mince, sage, sugar, salt and pepper. Mix thoroughly.

Roll the pork mixture into a ball. Using a sheet of greaseproof paper, flatten the mince into a thin, circular patty, slightly bigger than the size of an English muffin. Cover and place in the coldest part of the fridge for 1–2 hours. Alternatively, prepare the sausage patty the night before and leave in the fridge overnight, ready to be cooked in the morning.

Heat a little oil in a frying pan over a low-medium heat. Place the sausage patty into the pan and cook for around 3 minutes per side, or until cooked through and golden.

Drain any excess oil and remove the sausage from the pan. Serve with pancakes and scrambled eggs as part of a 'big breakfast', or as part of a sausage and egg muffin.

BREAKFAST PANCAKES

(AMERICAN FAST-FOOD STYLE)

Makes 8 Pancakes

120 g/4 oz self raising flour
Pinch of salt
30 g/1 oz caster sugar
1 egg
142 ml/¼ pint milk

In a large bowl, combine the self raising flour and salt. Add the sugar and mix well.

In a separate bowl, combine the egg and milk. Combine with the dry ingredients and whisk thoroughly to create a smooth, thin batter. Add a little more milk if necessary.

Lightly grease a frying pan with vegetable oil and heat to medium-high.

Drop one ladleful of the pancake batter into the pan at a time, tilting the pan to spread the mixture into a medium sized pancake. Allow the pancake to cook for 50–60 seconds or until bubbles cover the pancake.

Use a flat spatula to flip the pancake over and continue to cook on the other side for a further 30–40 seconds.

Remove from the pan and set aside.

Continue the process until all of the pancakes are cooked.

The pancakes can be served as part of a 'big breakfast' with scrambled eggs and American breakfast sausage, or simply with cooked bacon and maple syrup.

MEATBALL SUB
(Deli-Sandwich Style)

Serves 1

This recipe makes enough meatballs and marinara sauce for three sandwiches. The meatballs and sauce freeze well for up to 3 months.

2 slices of white bread, crusts removed
½ teaspoon dried Italian herbs
2 cloves of garlic
1 teaspoon dried parsley
2 teaspoons grated Parmesan cheese
1 egg
500 g/1.1 lb beef mince
1 large French baguette or sub roll
1 processed cheese slice (optional)

For the Marinara Sauce:
1 tablespoon olive oil
1 clove of garlic
1 x 400g tin of chopped tomatoes
50 ml/2 fl oz water
1 teaspoon dried Italian herbs
1 teaspoon sugar
¼ teaspoon salt
Pinch of black pepper

In a blender, combine the white bread, Italian herbs, garlic, parsley and Parmesan cheese.

Add the blended mixture to a large bowl along with the egg and beef mince. Mix thoroughly until well combined. Shape into 10–12 balls and arrange on a baking tray, leaving a little space between each meatball.

Preheat the oven to 180°C/350°F/Gas Mark 4.

Place the tray of meatballs onto the middle shelf of the oven and cook for around 20 minutes, or until cooked through.

In a separate pan, heat a little olive oil.

Finely chop the clove of garlic and stir-fry on a low heat for 1–2 minutes.

Add the tinned chopped tomatoes, water, dried Italian herbs, sugar, salt and pepper.

Bring the sauce to a boil, reduce the heat to low and simmer for 15–20 minutes, stirring occasionally.

When the meatballs are cooked, lift them from the baking tray and place them into the pan. Mix carefully to coat the meatballs with the marinara sauce.

Split the baguette or sub roll.

Place 3–4 meatballs onto the roll with a little sauce.

Add the cheese slice if desired and place the sandwich under a hot grill for 2–3 minutes.

Allow the sandwich to rest for 2 minutes and serve.

CHICKEN FAJITA WRAP

(MEXICAN/AMERICAN FAST-FOOD STYLE)

Serves 1–2

Spicy, succulent pan-fried chicken strips with onion and peppers, wrapped in a soft flour tortilla. The optional processed cheese slice is a modern day American fast-food addition to this classic Mexican dish.

1 tablespoon cornflour
¼ chicken stock cube, crumbled
½ teaspoon dried oregano
1 teaspoon chilli powder
½ teaspoon cayenne pepper
1 teaspoon paprika
¼ teaspoon garlic powder
½ teaspoon onion powder
¼ teaspoon cumin powder
1 teaspoon sugar
¼ teaspoon salt
Pinch of black pepper
1 large skinless, boneless chicken breast fillet (around
    113 g/4 oz weight)
2 tablespoons vegetable oil
½ green pepper, finely sliced
1 onion, finely sliced
2 tablespoons lime juice
50 ml/2 fl oz water
1 processed cheese slice (optional)
2 large flour tortillas

In a small bowl, combine the cornflour, chicken stock cube, oregano, chilli powder, cayenne pepper, paprika, garlic powder, onion powder, cumin powder, sugar, salt and black pepper. Mix thoroughly.

Trim any excess fat from the breast fillet and cut into 5–6 long strips.

Heat the vegetable oil over a medium-high heat. Add the sliced green pepper and onion and stir-fry for 3–4 minutes. Remove from the pan and set aside.

Add a little more vegetable oil to the pan if necessary. Add the chicken breast strips and stir-fry for 1–2 minutes. Add 1 tablespoon of the prepared fajita mix (or to taste) and mix well.

Add the lime juice and water. Return the green pepper and onion to the pan.

Mix well and continue to stir-fry for a further 3–4 minutes or until the chicken is cooked through and the sauce begins to thicken.

If desired, cut the processed cheese slice in half. Arrange half of the cheese on each flour tortilla.

Add a generous amount of the chicken, green pepper and onions. Fold and roll the fajita wraps. Serve with Guacamole (page 137), sour cream and Pico De Gallo (page 138).

CHAR GRILLED CHICKEN SANDWICH

(DELI-SANDWICH STYLE)

Serves 1

1 large skinless, boneless chicken breast fillet (around
    113 g/4 oz weight)
1 tablespoon olive oil
Pinch of salt
Pinch of black pepper
1 tablespoon poppy seeds
2 tablespoons mayonnaise
½ teaspoon honey
½ teaspoon Dijon mustard
2 slices of granary or wholemeal bread
4 tomato slices
4 cucumber slices
1 handful of shredded lettuce

Preheat the oven to 190°C/375°F/Gas Mark 5.

Heat a griddle pan to a high heat. Cover the chicken breast fillet with olive oil, salt and pepper. Place the chicken fillet onto the hot griddle pan and cook for 2–3 minutes. Turn the chicken breast over and cook on the other side for a further 2–3 minutes.

Lift the chicken breast off the griddle pan and place it on a baking tray. Place the tray onto the middle shelf and cook for a further 15–20 minutes or until cooked through.

Remove the cooked chicken from the oven and set aside to cool.

Heat a dry, flat frying pan on a medium heat. Add the poppy seeds and toast in the pan for 1–2 minutes, stirring occasionally. Remove the seeds from the pan and set aside to cool.

In a small bowl, combine the mayonnaise, honey and Dijon mustard. Mix thoroughly. Spread the mixture generously on both slices of the bread.

Slice the chicken into strips and add to the sandwich. Add a little extra honey mustard mayonnaise on top of the chicken pieces and sprinkle with the toasted poppy seeds. Add the tomato slices, cucumber slices and shredded lettuce.

Add the remaining bread slice, cut the sandwich into two triangles and serve.

CORONATION CHICKEN SUB

(Deli-Sandwich Style)

Serves 1

1 large skinless, boneless chicken breast fillet (around
  113 g/4 oz weight)
1 tablespoon olive oil
Pinch of salt
Pinch of black pepper
5–6 tablespoons mayonnaise
1 teaspoon mango chutney (optional)
1 teaspoon mild Madras curry powder
Pinch of chilli powder
1 tablespoon lemon juice
1 large sub roll or French baguette
4 tomato slices
4 cucumber slices
1 handful of shredded lettuce
¼ red onion, finely chopped

Preheat the oven to 190°C/375°F/Gas Mark 5.

Place the chicken breast fillet onto a baking tray and cover with olive
oil, salt and pepper. Cover loosely with foil and place on the middle shelf
of the oven for 25–30 minutes. Remove the foil after 15 minutes.

Remove the cooked chicken from the oven and set aside to cool.

In a small bowl, combine the mayonnaise, mango chutney if desired,
curry powder, chilli powder and lemon juice.

When the cooked chicken breast is fully cooled, cut it into small pieces.
Add the prepared sauce and mix well.

Refrigerate the chicken and sauce together for at least 2 hours to allow
the flavours to combine.

Slice the baguette or sub roll and fill with the coronation chicken. Add
the tomato slices, cucumber slices and shredded lettuce. Sprinkle with
the chopped red onion and serve.

CHEESE AND ONION SANDWICH

(DELI-SANDWICH STYLE)

Serves 1

½ small onion, finely chopped
40 g/1½ oz grated Cheddar cheese
1–2 tablespoons mayonnaise
1 tablespoon finely chopped chives (optional)
2 slices of white bread

In a bowl, combine the chopped onion, grated Cheddar cheese and mayonnaise. Mix well, adding more mayonnaise if necessary. Add the chopped chives if desired.

Spread one slice of the bread generously with the prepared cheese and onion mixture.

Add the remaining bread slice, cut the sandwich into two triangles and serve.

TUNA MAYONNAISE SANDWICH
(Deli-Sandwich Style)

Serves 1

The lemon juice in this recipe does not come through strongly in the finished sandwich but helps to add a fresh flavour and cut the strength of the tinned tuna. If desired, add tinned sweetcorn through the tuna mayonnaise to give extra crunch to your sandwich. Alternatively, add thin slices of cucumber for a further burst of freshness.

1 x 185g tin of tuna in spring water
3 tablespoons mayonnaise (recommended brand: Hellman's)
2 teaspoons lemon juice
Pinch of salt
2 slices of granary or wholemeal bread

Drain the tuna and squeeze dry. Add the mayonnaise, lemon juice and salt. Mix thoroughly and set aside in the refrigerator for at least 1 hour or until well chilled.

Spread half of the tuna mayonnaise mixture onto one slice of bread. Add the remaining bread slice, divide the sandwich into triangles and serve.

BLT SANDWICH
(DELI-SANDWICH STYLE)

Serves 1

The ultimate bacon sandwich, garnished with lettuce, tomato slices and mayonnaise.

4 slices of smoked bacon
2 large slices of white bread
1 tablespoon mayonnaise
4 large tomato slices
1 handful of shredded iceberg lettuce
Pinch of black pepper

Grill the smoked bacon slices under a medium-hot grill for 4–6 minutes or until cooked to preference. Turn the bacon half way through cooking. Set aside.

Toast the bread slices until just golden and set aside to cool.

Spread half of the mayonnaise on each slice.

Place the tomato slices and shredded lettuce onto one slice of bread. Add black pepper, then place the bacon slices on top.

Add the remaining bread layer and press down gently. Divide the sandwich into triangles and serve.

ALL DAY BREAKFAST SUB

(Deli-Sandwich Style)

Serves 1

Use any good quality pork sausage you like in this sandwich. Any good bacon will also work well, however sweet cured bacon is preferred by many sandwich bars as it combines well with the mayonnaise and ketchup in the sandwich.

1 large pork sausage
2 slices of sweet cured bacon
1 egg
1 tablespoon mayonnaise (recommended brand: Hellman's)
1 sub roll or baguette
1 tablespoon tomato ketchup (recommended brand: Heinz)
3–4 tomato slices

Fry the sausage and bacon in a little vegetable oil over a medium heat for 7–8 minutes or until fully cooked. Slice the sausage lengthwise. Set aside.

Heat a small pan filled with water until boiling. Add the egg and boil for 6 minutes. Rinse and peel the egg, submerged in cold water.

Break the egg with a fork and mash well with the mayonnaise.

Slice the sub roll or baguette. Spread the tomato ketchup over the inside. Add the mashed egg mayonnaise, sliced sausage and bacon. Add the tomato slices and serve.

10

DRINKS AND DESSERTS

The indulgence of takeaways is a perfect time to go that extra mile and indulge in a tasty dessert. As the calories increase, so do the prices however, with many takeaway dessert menus charging increasingly high prices for simple items such as ice cream or chocolate chip cookies.

The following recipes will provide delicious drinks to accompany any of the meals in this book, and a variety of desserts to complete the meal. The sweetest part of course being that by creating your own, you'll pay only a fraction of the price. Unfortunately, the calories still count the same!

VANILLA MILKSHAKE

(AMERICAN FAST-FOOD STYLE)

Serves 1

200 ml/7 fl oz vanilla ice cream
125ml/4 fl oz semi-skimmed milk
4 teaspoons white sugar

In a blender, combine the vanilla ice cream, semi-skimmed milk and sugar.

Blitz well until fully combined. Add more sugar to taste if desired and serve.

VARIATIONS

CHOCOLATE MILKSHAKE

Replace the 4 teaspoons of white sugar with 1 tablespoon of chocolate flavour milkshake powder.

STRAWBERRY MILKSHAKE

Replace the 4 teaspoons of white sugar with 1½ tablespoons of strawberry flavour milkshake powder.

LASSI

(Indian Restaurant Style)

Serves 1

Reaching for a pint of water is a common mistake amongst rookie curry fans. Doing so is more likely to clean the taste buds, resulting in them being ever more alert to the heat from the spices! A yogurt or milk based drink is preferred and this recipe will provide the perfect partner to any spicy curry.

100 ml/3½ fl oz natural yogurt
200 ml/7 fl oz ice-cold water
Pinch of salt
2 teaspoons caster sugar
1 green cardamom pod
Fresh mint for garnish

In a blender, combine the natural yogurt, cold water, salt and caster sugar.

Lightly crush the cardamom pod, remove the seeds from inside and add to the blender.

Blitz well again until the mixture becomes frothy on top.

Pour into a glass or serving jug and garnish with 1–2 sprigs of fresh mint. Serve with any Indian curry.

HOT CHOCOLATE

(AMERICAN FAST-FOOD STYLE)

Serves 1

This easy hot chocolate can be served with grated dark chocolate or marshmallows, or simply on its own to warm up a cold night.

½ tablespoon cocoa powder
½ tablespoon sugar
1 tablespoon water
½ cinnamon stick
230 ml/8 fl oz semi-skimmed milk
Dash of vanilla extract

In a serving bowl or cup, combine the cocoa powder, sugar and water. Mix well until a paste is formed.

Add the cinnamon stick and semi-skimmed milk to a small pan. Heat the milk over a medium heat until it just comes to the boil.

Strain the milk through a sieve and combine with the cocoa powder, sugar and water mixture. Mix well until all of the ingredients are fully combined.

Add the vanilla extract, stir through and serve.

CHOCOLATE CHIP COOKIES

(DELI-STYLE)

Makes 10–12 Cookies

Chewy cookies, packed with chocolate chips. Serve with coffee for brunch or with ice cold milk for a late supper. Replace 50 g/2 oz of the self raising flour with 50 g/2 oz of cocoa powder if desired. The cookie dough freezes well and can be used immediately if shaped before freezing.

125 g/4 oz butter
100 g/3½ oz caster sugar
100 g/3½ oz light brown sugar
1 egg
1 teaspoon vanilla extract
225 g/8 oz self raising flour
½ teaspoon salt
100 g/3½ oz chocolate chips

In a large bowl, combine the butter, caster sugar and brown sugar. Mix thoroughly until the butter and sugar are well combined.

Add the egg and vanilla extract and mix thoroughly once more.

Add the flour, salt and chocolate chips. Mix well and shape into a long log shape. Refrigerate the dough for 2 hours.

Preheat the oven to 180°C/350°F/Gas Mark 4.

Remove the cookie dough from the fridge and slice into individual cookies. Bake the cookies for 7–8 minutes or until just cooked through. Allow an extra 3–4 minutes if using frozen cookie dough.

Remove the finished cookies from the oven and leave to rest for 2–3 minutes. The cookies will be very soft when removed from the oven but should become slightly more firm as they cool down. Serve immediately or place on a wire rack to cool completely.

VANILLA ICE CREAM

(ITALIAN RESTAURANT STYLE)

Serves 2–3

This homemade ice cream will rival the finest restaurant bought variety, made soft with semi-skimmed milk.

120 ml/4 fl oz semi-skimmed milk
50 g/2 oz white sugar
2 teaspoons vanilla extract
120 ml/4 fl oz double cream

In a bowl, combine the semi-skimmed milk, white sugar and vanilla extract. Mix well.

In a separate bowl, whisk the cream until it becomes thick.

Add the cream to the milk and sugar mixture and mix well once again.

Pour the mixture into an ice cream maker and churn as per instructions.

Alternatively, make the ice cream by hand. Place the mixture into a freezer-proof tub and place in the freezer. After 40 minutes, stir the mixture well, breaking up any ice crystals which may have formed. Mix until the mixture becomes smooth again.

Place the tub back in the freezer and repeat the mixing process every 40–45 minutes until the ice cream is completely smooth and frozen. At this stage the mixture can be frozen as normal until needed.

Serve with hot chocolate sauce or simply with wafers.

EASY CHOCOLATE CHEESECAKE
(Deli-Style)

Serves 2

This instant chocolate cheesecake uses only four ingredients and can be prepared in just a few minutes.

4 digestive biscuits
2 tablespoons butter
3 tablespoons chocolate and hazelnut spread (recommended brand: Nutella)
2 tablespoons soft cheese

Add the digestive biscuits to a blender and blitz into crumbs.

Melt the butter and slowly combine it with the biscuit crumbs. Press the mixture into a dessert ring and pat down firmly.

In a bowl, combine the chocolate and hazelnut spread and soft cheese. Mix well. Taste and add more chocolate or cheese to taste.

Spoon the chocolate and cheese mixture onto the top of the biscuit base. Refrigerate for 2–3 hours or until set.

Remove the dessert ring carefully, slice and serve.

BANANA MUFFINS

(Deli-Style)

Makes 12–14 Muffins

These muffins freeze extremely well, making them ideal to defrost each night and take to work the following day.

180 g/6 oz plain flour
1 teaspoon baking powder
1 teaspoon baking soda
½ teaspoon salt
3 ripe bananas
150 g/5 oz white sugar
1 egg
1 teaspoon vanilla extract
75 ml/2½ fl oz vegetable oil

In a large bowl, combine the plain flour, baking powder, baking soda and salt. Mix well.

In a separate bowl, mash the bananas and add the sugar, egg, vanilla extract and oil. Mix well.

Add the wet ingredients to the dry ingredients and mix thoroughly until well combined.

Preheat the oven to 190°C/375°F/Gas Mark 5.

Lightly oil two muffin trays. Pour a large tablespoon of the mixture into each muffin space.

Bake for 18–20 minutes. Check that the muffins are completely cooked by piercing the centre of a muffin with a fork. The muffins are ready when the fork comes out clean.

Remove the muffins from the oven and leave to rest for 5 minutes before removing from the trays and arranging on a wire rack to cool completely.

The muffins will freeze well for up to 1 month.

INDEX

Three ways to order *Right Way* books:

1. Visit www.constablerobinson.com and order through our website.

2. Telephone the TBS order line on 01206 255 800.
    Order lines are open Monday – Friday, 8:30am – 5:30pm.

3. Use this order form and send a cheque made payable to TBS Ltd or charge my
    [ ] Visa   [ ] Mastercard   [ ] Maestro (issue no   )

Card number: _____

Expiry date: _____ Last three digits on back of card: _____

Signature: _____

(your signature is essential when paying by credit or debit card)

No. of copies	Title	Price	Total
	The Curry Secret	£5.99	
	The New Curry Secret	£7.99	
	Thai Cookery Secrets	£5.99	
	Chinese Cookery Secrets	£5.99	
	For P&P add £2.75 for the first book, 60p for each additional book		
	Grand Total		£

Name: _____

Address: _____

_____ Postcode: _____

Daytime Tel. No./Email _____
(in case of query)

**Please return forms to Cash Sales/Direct Mail Dept., The Book
Service, Colchester Road, Frating Green, Colchester CO7 7DW.**

Enquiries to readers@constablerobinson.com.

Constable and Robinson Ltd (directly or via its agents) may mail, email or
phone you about promotions or products.

[ ] Tick box if you do not want these from us [ ] or our subsidiaries.

www.constablerobinson.com/rightway